Magical Passes

Magical Passes

The Practical Wisdom of the Shamans of Ancient Mexico

CARLOS
CASTANEDA

HarperCollins*Publishers*

Photographs by Photo Vision and Graphics, Van Nuys, California

The two practitioners of Tensegrity demonstrating the magical passes are Kylie Lundahl and Miles Reid.

FIRST EDITION

Designed by Jessica Shatan

Library of Congress Cataloging-in-Publication Data

Castaneda, Carlos
    Magical Passes : the practical wisdom of the Shamans of ancient Mexico /
Carlos Castaneda : photographs by Photo Vision and Graphics in Van Nuys,
California. — 1st ed.
        p.   cm.
    ISBN 0-06-017584-2
    1. Shamanism—Mexico.   2. Exercise—Religious aspects.   3. Juan, Don, 1891– .
4. Castaneda, Carlos.   5. Mexico—Religion.   6. Indians of Mexico—Religion.
I. Title.
BF1622.M6C37   1998   97-26884

98 99 00 01 02 ❖/RRD 10 9 8 7 6 5 4 3 2 1

To every one of the practitioners of Tensegrity,
who, by rallying their forces around it,
have put me in touch with energetic formulations
that were never available to
don Juan Matus or the shamans of his lineage

CONTENTS

Magical Passes

INTRODUCTION

Don Juan Matus, a master sorcerer, a *nagual*, as master sorcerers are called when they lead a group of other sorcerers, introduced me to the cognitive world of shamans who lived in Mexico in ancient times. Don Juan Matus was an Indian who was born in Yuma, Arizona. His father was a Yaqui Indian from Sonora, Mexico, and his mother was presumably a Yuma Indian from Arizona. Don Juan lived in Arizona until he was ten years old. He was then taken by his father to Sonora, Mexico, where they were caught in the endemic Yaqui wars against the Mexicans. His father was killed, and as a ten-year-old child don Juan ended up in Southern Mexico, where he grew up with relatives.

At the age of twenty, he came in contact with a master sorcerer. His name was Julian Osorio. He introduced don Juan into a lineage of sorcerers that was purported to be twenty-five generations long. He was not an Indian at all, but the son of European immigrants to Mexico. Don Juan related to me that the *nagual* Julian had been an actor, and that he was a dashing person—a raconteur, a mime, adored by everybody, influential, commanding. In one of his theatrical tours to the provinces, the actor Julian Osorio fell under the influence of another *nagual*, Elias Ulloa, who transmitted to him the knowledge of his lineage of sorcerers.

Don Juan Matus, following the tradition of his lineage of shamans, taught some bodily movements which he called *magical passes* to his four disciples: Taisha Abelar, Florinda Donner-Grau, Carol Tiggs, and myself. He taught them to us in the same spirit in which they had been taught for generations, with one notable departure: he eliminated the excessive ritual which had surrounded the teaching and performance of those magical passes for generations. Don Juan's comments in this respect were that ritual had lost its impetus as new generations of practitioners became more interested in efficiency and functionalism. He recommended to me, however, that under no circumstances should I talk about the magical passes with any of his disciples or with people in general. His reasons were that the magical passes pertained exclusively to each person, and that their effect was so shattering, it was better just to practice them without discussing them.

Don Juan Matus taught me everything he knew about the sorcerers of his lineage. He stated, asserted, affirmed, explained to me every nuance of his knowledge. Therefore, everything I say about the magical passes is a direct result of his instruction. The magical passes were not invented. They were discovered by the shamans of don Juan's lineage who lived in Mexico in ancient times, while they were in shamanistic states of *heightened awareness*. The discovery of the magical passes was quite accidental. It began as very simple queries about the nature of an incredible sensation of well-being that those shamans experienced in those states of *heightened awareness* when they held certain bodily positions, or when they moved their limbs in some specific manner. Their sensation of well-being had been so intense that their drive to repeat those movements in their normal awareness became the focus of all their endeavors.

By all appearances, they succeeded in their task, and found themselves the possessors of a very complex series of movements that, when practiced, yielded them tremendous results in terms of mental and physical prowess. In fact, the results of performing these movements were so dramatic that they called them *magical passes*. They taught them for generations only to shaman initiates, on a personal basis, following elaborate rituals and secret ceremonies.

Don Juan Matus, in teaching the magical passes, departed radically from tradition. Such a departure forced don Juan to reformulate the pragmatic goal of the magical passes. He presented this goal to me not so much as the enhancement of mental and physical balance, as it had been in the past, but as the practical possibility of *redeploying energy*. He explained that such a departure was due to the influence of the two *naguals* who had preceded him.

It was the belief of the sorcerers of don Juan's lineage that there is an inherent amount of energy existing in each one of us, an amount which is not subject to the onslaughts of outside forces for augmenting it or for decreasing it. They believed that this quantity of energy was sufficient to accomplish something which those sorcerers deemed to be the obsession of every man on Earth: breaking the parameters of normal perception. Don Juan Matus was convinced that our incapacity to break those parameters was induced by our culture and social milieu. He maintained that our culture and social milieu deployed every bit of our inherent energy in fulfilling established behavioral patterns which didn't allow us to break those parameters of normal perception.

"Why in the world would I, or anyone else, want to break those parameters?" I asked don Juan on one occasion.

"Breaking those parameters is the unavoidable issue of mankind," he replied. "Breaking them means the entrance into unthinkable worlds of a pragmatic value in no way different from the value of our world of everyday life. Regardless of whether or not we accept this premise, we are obsessed with breaking those parameters, and we fail miserably at it, hence the profusion of drugs and stimulants and religious rituals and ceremonies among modern man."

"Why do you think we have failed so miserably, don Juan?" I asked.

"Our failure to fulfill our subliminal wish," he said, "is due to the fact that we tackle it in a helter-skelter way. Our tools are too crude. They are equivalent to trying to bring down a wall by ramming it with the head. Man never considers this breakage in terms of energy. For sorcerers, success is determined only by the accessibility or the inaccessibility of energy.

"Since it is impossible," he continued, "to augment our inherent energy, the only avenue open for the sorcerers of ancient Mexico was the *redeployment* of that energy. For them, this process of *redeployment* began with the magical passes, and the way they affected the physical body."

Don Juan stressed in every way possible, while imparting his instruction, the fact that the enormous emphasis the shamans of his lineage had put on physical prowess and mental well-being had lasted to the present day. I was able to corroborate the truth of his statements by observing him and his fifteen sorcerer-companions. Their superb physical and mental balance was the most obvious feature about them.

Don Juan's reply when I once asked him directly why sorcerers put so much stock in the physical side of man was a total surprise to me. I had always thought that he himself was a spiritual man.

"Shamans are not spiritual at all," he said. "They are very practical beings. It is a well-known fact, however, that shamans are generally regarded as eccentric, or even insane. Perhaps that is what makes you think that they are spiritual. They seem insane because they are always trying to explain things that cannot be explained. In the course of such futile attempts to give complete explanations that cannot be completed under any circumstances, they lose all coherence and say inanities.

"You need a pliable body, if you want physical prowess and levelheadedness," he went on. "These are the two most important issues in the lives of shamans, because they bring forth sobriety and pragmatism: the only indispensable requisites for entering into other realms of perception. To navigate, in a genuine way, in the unknown necessitates an attitude of daring, but not one of recklessness. In order to establish a balance between audacity and recklessness, a sorcerer has to be extremely sober, cautious, skillful, and in superb physical condition."

"But why in superb physical condition, don Juan?" I asked. "Isn't the desire or the will to journey into the unknown enough?"

"Not in your pissy life!" he replied rather brusquely. "Just to conceive facing the unknown—much less enter into it—requires guts of steel, and a body that would be capable of holding those guts. What would be the point of being gutsy if you didn't have mental alertness, physical prowess, and adequate muscles?"

The superb physical condition that don Juan had steadily advocated from the first day of our association, the product of the rigorous execution of the magical passes, was, by all indications, the first step toward the *redeployment* of our inherent energy. This *redeployment of energy* was, in don Juan's view, the most crucial issue in the lives of shamans, as well as in the life of any individual. *Redeployment of energy* is a process which consists of transporting, from one place to another, energy which already exists within us. This energy has been displaced from centers of vitality in the body, which require that displaced energy in order to bring forth a balance between mental alertness and physical prowess.

The shamans of don Juan's lineage were deeply engaged with the *redeployment* of their inherent energy. This involvement wasn't an intellectual endeavor, nor was it the product of induction or deduction, or logical conclusions. It was the result of their ability to perceive energy as it flowed in the universe.

"Those sorcerers called this ability to perceive energy as it flowed in the universe *seeing*," don Juan explained to me. "They described *seeing* as a state of *heightened awareness* in which the human body is capable of perceiving energy as a flow, a current, a windlike vibration. To *see* energy as it flows in the universe is the product of a momentary halt of the system of interpretation proper to human beings."

"What is this system of interpretation, don Juan?" I asked.

"The shamans of ancient Mexico found out," he replied, "that every part of the human body is engaged, in one way or another, in turning this vibratory flow, this current of vibration, into some form of sensory input. The sum total of this bombardment of sensory input is then, through usage, turned into the system of interpretation that makes human beings capable of perceiving the world the way they do.

"To make this system of interpretation come to a halt," he went on, "was the result of tremendous discipline on the part of the sorcerers of ancient Mexico. They called this halt *seeing*, and made it the cornerstone of their knowledge. To *see* energy as it flowed in the universe was, for them, an essential tool that they employed in making their classificatory schemes. Because of this capacity, for instance, they conceived the total universe available to the perception of human beings as an onionlike affair, consisting of thousands of layers. The daily world of human beings, they believed, is but one such layer. Consequently, they also believed that other layers are not only accessible to human perception, but are part of man's natural heritage."

Another issue of tremendous value in the knowledge of those sorcerers, an issue which was also a consequence of their capacity to *see* energy as it flowed in the universe, was the discovery of the human energetic configuration. This human energetic configuration was, for them, a conglomerate of energy fields agglutinated together by a vibratory force that bound those energy fields into a *luminous ball* of energy. For the sorcerers of don Juan's lineage, a human being has an oblong shape like an egg, or a round shape like a ball. Thus, they called them *luminous eggs* or *luminous balls*. This sphere of luminosity was considered by them to be our true self—true in the sense that it is irreducible in terms of energy. It is irreducible because the totality of human resources are engaged in the act of perceiving it directly as energy.

Those shamans discovered that on the back face of this *luminous ball* there is a point of greater brilliance. They figured out, through processes of observing energy directly, that this point is key in the act of turning energy into sensory data and then interpreting it. For this reason, they called it the *assemblage point,* and deemed that perception is indeed assembled there. They described the *assemblage point* as being located behind the shoulder blades, an arm's length away from them. They also found out that the *assemblage point* for the entire human race is located on the same spot, thus giving every human being an entirely similar view of the world.

A finding of tremendous value for them, and for shamans of succeeding generations, was that the location of the *assemblage point* on that spot is the result of usage and socialization. For this reason, they considered it to be an arbitrary position which gives merely the illusion of being final and irreducible. A product of this illusion is the seemingly unshakable conviction of human beings that the world they deal with daily is the only world that exists, and that its finality is undeniable.

"Believe me," don Juan said to me once, "this sense of finality about the world is a mere illusion. Due to the fact that it has never been challenged, it stands as the only possible view. To *see* energy as it flows in the universe is the tool for challenging it. Through the use of this tool, the sorcerers of my lineage arrived at the conclusion that there are indeed a staggering number of worlds available to man's perception. They described those worlds as being all-inclusive realms, realms where one can act and struggle. In other words, they are worlds where one can live and die, as in this world of everyday life."

During the thirteen years of my association with him, don Juan taught me the basic steps toward accomplishing this feat of *seeing.* I have discussed those steps in all of my previous writings, but never have I touched on the key point in this process: the magical passes. He taught me a great number of them, but along with that wealth of knowledge, don Juan also left me with the certainty that I was the last link of his lineage. Accepting that I was the last link of his lineage implied automatically for me the task of finding new ways to disseminate the knowledge of his lineage, since its continuity was no longer an issue.

I need to clarify a very important point in this regard: Don Juan Matus was not ever interested in teaching his knowledge; he was interested in perpetuating his lineage. His three other disciples and I were the means—chosen, he said, by the spirit itself, for he had no active part in it—that were going to ensure that perpetuation. Therefore, he engaged himself in a titanic effort to teach me all he knew about sorcery, or shamanism, and about the development of his lineage.

In the course of training me, he realized that my energetic configuration was, according to him, so vastly different from his own that it couldn't mean anything else but the end of his line. I told him that I resented enormously his interpretation of whatever invisible difference existed between us. I didn't like the burden of being the last of his line, nor did I understand his reasoning.

"The shamans of ancient Mexico," he said to me once, "believed that choice, as human beings understand it, is the precondition of the cognitive world of man, but that it is only a benevolent interpretation of something which is found when awareness ventures beyond the cushion of our world, a benevolent interpretation of acquiescence. Human beings are in the throes of forces that pull them every which way. The art of sorcerers is not really to choose, but to be subtle enough to acquiesce.

"Sorcerers, although they seem to make nothing else but decisions, make no decisions at all," he went on. "I didn't decide to choose you, and I didn't decide that you would be the way you are. Since I couldn't choose to whom I would impart my knowledge, I had to accept whomever the spirit was offering me. And that person was you, and you are energetically capable only of ending, not of continuing."

He maintained that the ending of his line had nothing to do with him or his efforts, or with his success or failure as a sorcerer seeking total freedom. He understood it as something that had to do with a choice exercised beyond the human level, not by beings or entities, but by the impersonal forces of the universe.

Finally, I came to accept what don Juan called my fate. Accepting it put me face to face with another issue that he referred to as *locking the door when you leave*. That is to say, I assumed the responsibility of deciding exactly what to do with everything he had taught me and carrying out my decision impeccably. First of all, I asked myself the crucial question of what to do with the magical passes: the facet of don Juan's knowledge most imbued with pragmatism and function. I decided to use the magical passes and teach them to whoever wanted to learn them. My decision to end the secrecy that had surrounded them for an undetermined length of time was, naturally, the corollary of my total conviction that I am indeed the end of don Juan's lineage. It became inconceivable to me that I should carry secrets which were not even mine. To shroud the magical passes in secrecy was not my decision. It was my decision, however, to end such a condition.

I endeavored from then on to come up with a more generic form of each magical pass, a form suitable to everyone. This resulted in a configuration of slightly modified forms of each one of the magical passes. I have called this new configuration of movements *Tensegrity*, a term which belongs to architecture, where it means "the property of skeleton structures that employ continuous tension members and discontinuous compression members in such a way that each member operates with the maximum efficiency and economy."

In order to explain what the magical passes of the sorcerers who lived in Mexico in ancient times are, I would like to make a clarification: "ancient times" meant, for don Juan, a time ten thousand years ago and beyond, a figure that seems incongruous if examined from the point of view of the classificatory schemes of modern scholars. When I confronted don Juan with the discrepancy between his estimate and what I considered to be a more realistic one, he remained adamant in his conviction. He believed it to be a fact that people who lived in the New World ten thousand years ago were deeply concerned with matters of the universe and perception that modern man has not even begun to fathom.

Regardless of our differing chronological interpretations, the effectiveness of the magical passes is undeniable to me, and I feel obligated to elucidate the subject strictly following the manner in which it was presented to me. The directness of their effect on me has had a deep influence on the way in which I deal with them. What I am presenting in this work is an intimate reflection of that influence.

Magical Passes

The first time don Juan talked to me at length about magical passes was when he made a derogatory comment about my weight.

"You are way too chubby," he said, looking at me from head to toe and shaking his head in disapproval. "You are one step from being fat. Wear and tear is beginning to show in you. Like any other member of your race, you are developing a lump of fat on your neck, like a bull. It's time that you take seriously one of the sorcerers' greatest findings: the magical passes."

"What magical passes are you talking about, don Juan?" I asked. "You have never mentioned this topic to me before. Or, if you have, it must have been so lightly that I can't recall anything about it."

"Not only have I told you a great deal about magical passes," he said, "you know a great number of them already. I have been teaching them to you all along."

As far as I was concerned, it wasn't true that he had taught me any magical passes all along. I protested vehemently.

"Don't be so passionate about defending your wonderful self," he joked, making a ridiculous gesture of apology with his eyebrows. "What I meant to say is that you imitate everything I do, so I have been cashing in on your imitation capacity. I have shown you various magical passes, all along, and you have always taken them to be my delight in cracking my joints. I like the way you interpret them: cracking my joints! We are going to keep on referring to them in that manner.

"I have shown you ten different ways of cracking my joints," he continued. "Each one of them is a magical pass that fits to perfection my body and yours. You could say that those ten magical passes are in your line and mine. They belong to us personally and individually, as they belonged to other sorcerers who were just like the two of us in the twenty-five generations that preceded us."

The magical passes don Juan was referring to, as he himself had said, were ways in which I thought he cracked his joints. He used to move his arms, legs, torso, and hips in specific ways, I thought, in order to create a maximum stretch of his muscles, bones, and ligaments. The result of these stretching movements, from my point of view, was a succession of cracking sounds which I always thought that he was producing for my amazement and amusement. He, indeed, had asked me time and time again to imitate him. In a challenging manner, he had even dared me to memorize the movements and repeat them at home until I could get my joints to make cracking noises, just like his.

I had never succeeded in reproducing the sounds, yet I had definitely but unwittingly learned all the movements. I know now that not achieving that cracking sound was a blessing in disguise, because the muscles and tendons of the arms and back should *never* be stressed to that point. Don Juan was born with a facility to crack the joints of his arms and back, just as some people have the facility to crack their knuckles.

"How did the old sorcerers invent those magical passes, don Juan?" I asked.

"Nobody invented them," he said sternly. "To think that they were invented implies instantly the intervention of the mind, and this is not the case when it comes to those magical passes. They were, rather, discovered by the old shamans. I was told that it all began with the extraordinary sensation of well-being that those shamans experienced when they were in shamanistic states of *heightened awareness*. They felt such tremendous, enthralling vigor that they struggled to repeat it in their hours of vigil.

"At first," don Juan explained to me once, "those shamans believed that it was a mood of well-being that *heightened awareness* created in general. Soon, they found out that not all the states of shamanistic *heightened awareness* which they entered produced in them the same sensation of well-being. A more careful scrutiny revealed to them that whenever that sensation of well-being occurred, they had always been engaged in some specific kind of bodily movement. They realized that while they were in states of *heightened awareness*, their bodies moved involuntarily in certain ways, and that those certain ways were indeed the cause of that unusual sensation of physical and mental plenitude."

Don Juan speculated that it had always appeared to him that the movements that the bodies of those shamans executed automatically in *heightened awareness* were a sort of hidden heritage of mankind, something that had been put in deep storage, to be revealed only to those who were looking for it. He portrayed those sorcerers as deep-sea divers, who without knowing it, reclaimed it.

Don Juan said that those sorcerers arduously began to piece together some of the movements they remembered. Their efforts paid off. They were capable of re-creating movements that had seemed to them to be automatic reactions of the body in a state of *heightened awareness*. Encouraged by their success, they were capable of re-creating hundreds of movements, which they performed without ever attempting to classify them into an understandable scheme. Their idea was that in *heightened awareness*, the movements happened spontaneously, and that there was a force that guided their effect, without the intervention of their volition.

Don Juan commented that the nature of their findings always led him to believe that the sorcerers of ancient times were extraordinary people, because the movements that they discovered were never revealed in the same fashion to modern shamans who also entered into *heightened awareness*. Perhaps this was because modern shamans had learned the movements beforehand, in some fashion or another, from their predecessors, or perhaps because the sorcerers of ancient times had more *energetic mass*.

"What do you mean, don Juan, that they had more *energetic mass?*" I asked. "Were they bigger men?"

"I don't think they were physically any bigger," he said, "but energetically, they appeared to the eye of a seer as an oblong shape. They called themselves *luminous eggs*. I have never *seen* a *luminous egg* in my life. All I have *seen* are *luminous balls*. It is presumable, then, that man has lost some *energetic mass* over the generations."

Don Juan explained to me that to a seer, the universe is composed of an infinite number of energy fields. They appear to the eye of the seer as luminous filaments that shoot out every which way. Don Juan said that those filaments crisscross through the *luminous balls* that human beings are, and that it was reasonable to assume that if human beings were once oblong shapes, like eggs, they were much higher than a ball. Therefore, energy fields that touched human beings at the crown of the *luminous egg* are no longer touching them now that they are *luminous balls*. Don Juan felt that this meant to him a loss of *energy mass*, which seemed to have been crucial for the purpose of reclaiming that hidden treasure: the magical passes.

"Why are the passes of the old shamans called magical passes, don Juan?" I asked him on one occasion.

"They are not just called magical passes," he said, "they are magical! They produce an effect that cannot be accounted for by means of ordinary explanations. These movements are not physical exercises or mere postures of the body; they are real attempts at reaching an optimal state of being.

"The *magic* of the movements," he went on, "is a subtle change that the practitioners experience on executing them. It is an ephemeral quality that the movement brings to their physical and mental states, a kind of shine, a light in the eyes. This subtle change is a *touch of the spirit*. It is as if the practitioners, through the movements, reestablish an unused link with the life force that sustains them."

He further explained that another reason that the movements are called *magical passes* is that by means of practicing them, shamans are transported, in terms of perception, to other states of being in which they can sense the world in an indescribable manner.

"Because of this quality, because of this magic," don Juan said to me, "the passes must be practiced not as exercises, but as a way of beckoning power."

"But can they be taken as physical movements, although they have never been taken as such?" I asked.

"You can practice them any way you wish," don Juan replied. "The magical passes enhance awareness, regardless of how you take them. The intelligent thing would be to take them as what they are: magical passes that on being practiced lead the practitioner to drop the mask of socialization."

"What is the mask of socialization?" I asked.

"The veneer that all of us defend and die for," he said. "The veneer we acquire in the world. The one that prevents us from reaching all our potential. The one that makes us believe we are immortal. The *intent* of thousands of sorcerers permeates these movements. Executing them, even in a casual way, makes the mind come to a halt."

"What do you mean that they make the mind come to a halt?" I asked.

"Everything that we do in the world," he said, "we recognize and identify by converting it into lines of similarity, lines of things that are strung together by purpose. For example, if I say to you *fork*, this immediately brings to your mind the idea of spoon, knife, tablecloth, napkin, plate, cup and saucer, glass of wine, chili con carne, banquet, birthday, fiesta. You could certainly go on naming things strung together by purpose, nearly forever. Everything we do is strung like this. The strange part for sorcerers is that they *see* that all these lines of affinity, all these lines of things strung together by purpose, are associated with man's idea that things are unchangeable and forever, like the word of God."

"I don't see, don Juan, why you bring the word of God into this elucidation. What does the word of God have to do with what you are trying to explain?"

"Everything!" he replied. "It seems to be that in our minds, the entire universe is like the word of God: absolute and unchanging. This is the way we conduct ourselves. In the depths of our minds, there is a checking device that doesn't permit us to stop to examine that the word of God, as we accept it and believe it to be, pertains to a dead world. A live world, on the other hand, is in constant flux. It moves. It changes. It reverses itself.

"The most abstract reason why the magical passes of the sorcerers of my lineage are magical," he went on, "is that in practicing them, the body of the practitioner realizes that everything, instead of being an unbroken chain of objects that have affinity for each other, is a current, a flux. And if everything in the universe is a flux, a current, that current can be stopped. A dam can be put on it, and in this manner, its flux can be halted or deviated."

Don Juan explained to me on one occasion the overall effect that the practice of the magical passes had on the sorcerers of his lineage, and correlated this effect with what would happen to modern practitioners.

"The sorcerers of my lineage," he said, "were shocked half to death upon realizing that practicing their magical passes brought about the halt of the otherwise uninterrupted flux of things. They constructed a series of metaphors to describe this halt, and in their effort to explain it, or reconsider it, they flubbed it. They lapsed into ritual and ceremony. They began to enact the act of halting the flux of things. They believed that if certain ceremonies and rituals were focused on a definite aspect of their magical passes, the magical passes themselves would beckon a specific result. Very soon, the number and complexity of their rituals and ceremonies became more encumbering than the number of their magical passes.

"It is very important," he went on, "to focus the attention of the practitioner on some definite aspect of the magical passes. However, that fixation should be light, funny, void of morbidity and grimness. It should be done for the hell of it, without really expecting returns."

He gave the example of one of his cohorts, a sorcerer by the name of Silvio Manuel, whose delight and predilection was to adapt the magical passes of the sorcerers of ancient times to the steps of his modern dancing. Don Juan described Silvio Manuel as a superb acrobat and dancer who actually danced the magical passes.

"The *nagual* Elias Ulloa," don Juan continued, "was the most prominent innovator of my lineage. He was the one who threw all the ritual out the window, so to speak, and practiced the magical passes exclusively for the purpose for which they were originally used at one time in the remote past: for the purpose of *redeploying energy*.

"The *nagual* Julian Osorio, who came after him," don Juan continued, "was the one who gave ritual the final death blow. Since he was a bona fide professional actor who at one time had made his living acting in the theater, he put enormous stock into what sorcerers called the *shamanistic theater*. He called it *the theater of infinity*, and into it, he poured all the magical passes that were available to him. Every movement of his characters was imbued to the gills with magical passes. Not only that, but he turned the theater into a new avenue for teaching them. Between the *nagual* Julian, the actor of *infinity*, and Silvio Manuel, the dancer of *infinity*, they had the whole thing pegged down. A new era was on the horizon! The era of pure *redeployment*!"

Don Juan's explanation of *redeployment* was that human beings, perceived as conglomerates of energy fields, are sealed energetic units that have definite boundaries which don't permit the entrance or the exit of energy. Therefore, the energy existing within that conglomerate of energy fields is all that each human individual can count on.

"The natural tendency of human beings," he said, "is to push energy away from the centers of vitality, which are located on the right side of the body, right at the edge of the rib cage on the area of the liver and gall-bladder; on the left side of the body, again, at the edge of the rib cage, on the area of the pancreas and spleen; on the back, right behind the other two centers, around the kidneys, and right above them, on the area of the adrenal glands; at the base of the neck on the V spot made by the sternum and clavicle; and around the uterus and ovaries in women."

"How do human beings push this energy away, don Juan?" I asked.

"By worrying," he replied. "By succumbing to the stress of everyday life. The duress of daily actions takes its toll on the body."

"And what happens to this energy, don Juan?" I asked.

"It gathers on the periphery of the *luminous ball*," he said, "sometimes to the point of making a thick barklike deposit. The magical passes relate to the total human being as a physical body, and as a conglomerate of energy fields. They agitate the energy that has been accumulated in the *luminous ball* and return it to the physical body itself. The magical passes engage both the body itself as a physical entity that suffers the dispersion of energy, and the body as an energetic entity which is capable of *redeploying* that dispersed energy.

"Having energy on the periphery of the *luminous ball*," he continued, "energy that is not being *redeployed*, is as useless as not having any energy at all. It is truly a terrifying situation to have a surplus of energy stashed away, inaccessible for all practical purposes. It is like being in the desert, dying of dehydration, while you carry a tank of water that you cannot open, because you don't have any tools. In that desert, you can't even find a rock to bang it with."

The true magic of the magical passes is the fact that they cause crusted-down energy to enter again into the centers of vitality, hence the feeling of well-being and prowess which is the practitioner's experience. The sorcerers of don Juan's lineage, before they entered into their excessive ritualism and ceremony, had formulated the basis for this *redeployment*. They called it *saturation*, meaning that they inundated their bodies with a profusion of magical passes, in order to allow the force that binds us together to guide those magical passes to cause the maximum *redeployment of energy*.

"But don Juan, are you telling me that every time you crack your joints, or every time I try to imitate you, we are really *redeploying energy?*" I asked him once, without really meaning to be sarcastic.

"Every time we execute a magical pass," he replied, "we are indeed altering the basic structures of our beings. Energy which is ordinarily crusted down is released and begins to enter into the vortexes of vitality of the body. Only by means of that reclaimed energy can we put up a dike, a barrier to contain an otherwise uncontainable and always deleterious flow."

I asked don Juan to give me an example of putting a dam on what he was calling a deleterious flow. I told him that I wanted to visualize it in my mind.

"I'll give you an example," he said. "For instance, at my age, I should be prey to high blood pressure. If I went to see a doctor, the doctor, upon seeing me, would assume that I must be an old Indian, plagued with uncertainties, frustrations, and bad diet; all of this, naturally, resulting in a most expected and predictable condition of high blood pressure: an acceptable corollary of my age.

"I don't have any problems with high blood pressure," he went on, "not because I am stronger than the average man or because of my genetic frame, but because my magical passes have made my body break through any patterns of behavior that result in high blood pressure. I can truthfully say that every time I crack my joints, following the execution of a magical pass, I am blocking off the flow of expectations and behavior that ordinarily result in high blood pressure at my age.

"Another example I can give you is the agility of my knees," he continued. "Haven't you noticed how much more agile I am than you? When it comes to moving my knees, I'm a kid! With my magical passes, I put a dam on the current of behavior and physicality that makes the knees of people, both men and women, stiff with age."

One of the most annoying feelings I had ever experienced was caused by the fact that don Juan Matus, although he could have been my grandfather, was infinitely younger than I. In comparison, I was stiff, opinionated, repetitious. I was senile. He, on the other hand, was fresh, inventive, agile, resourceful. In short, he possessed something which, although I was young, I did not: youth. He delighted in telling me repeatedly that young age was not youth, and that young age was in no way a deterrent to senility. He pointed out that if I watched my fellow men carefully and dispassionately, I would be able to corroborate that by the time they reached twenty years of age, they were already senile, repeating themselves inanely.

"How is it possible, don Juan," I said, "that you could be younger than I?"

"I have vanquished my mind," he said, opening his eyes wide to denote bewilderment. "I don't have a mind to tell me that it is time to be old. I don't honor agreements in which I didn't participate. Remember this: It is not just a slogan for sorcerers to say that they do not honor agreements in which they did not participate. To be plagued by old age is one such agreement."

We were silent for a long time. Don Juan seemed to be waiting, I thought, for the effect that his words might cause in me. What I thought to be my psychological unity was further ripped apart by a clearly dual response on my part. On one level, I repudiated with all my might the nonsense that don Juan was verbalizing; on another level, however, I couldn't fail to notice how accurate his remarks were. Don Juan was old, and yet he wasn't old at all. He was ages younger than I. He was free from encumbering thoughts and habit patterns. He was roaming around in incredible worlds. He was free, while I was imprisoned by heavy thought patterns and habits, by petty and futile considerations about myself, which I felt, on that occasion, for the first time ever, weren't even mine.

I asked don Juan on another occasion something that had been bothering me for a long time. He had stated that the sorcerers of ancient Mexico discovered the magical passes, which were some sort of hidden treasure, placed in storage for man to find. I wanted to know who would put something like that in storage for man. The only idea that I could come up with was derived from Catholicism. I thought of God doing it, or a guardian angel, or the Holy Spirit.

"It is not the Holy Spirit," he said, "which is only holy to you, because you're secretly a Catholic. And certainly it is not God, a benevolent father as you understand God. Nor is it a goddess, a nurturing mother, watching over the affairs of men, as many people believe to be the case. It is rather an impersonal force that has endless things in storage for those who dare to seek them. It is a force in the universe, like light or gravity. It is an agglutinating factor, a vibratory force that joins the conglomerate of energy fields that human beings are into one concise, cohesive unit. This vibratory force is the factor that doesn't allow the entrance or the exit of energy from the *luminous ball*.

"The sorcerers of ancient Mexico," he went on, "believed that the performance of their magical passes was the only factor that prepared and led the body to the transcendental corroboration of the existence of that agglutinating force."

From don Juan's explanations, I derived the conclusion that the vibratory force he spoke about, which agglutinates our fields of energy, is apparently similar to what modern-day astronomers believe must happen at the core of all the galaxies that exist in the cosmos. They believe that there, at their cores, a force of incalculable strength holds the stars of galaxies in place. This force, called a "black hole," is a theoretical construct which seems to be the most reasonable explanation as to why stars do not fly away, driven by their own rotational speeds.

Don Juan said that the old sorcerers knew that human beings, taken as conglomerates of energy fields, are held together not by energetic wrappings or energetic ligaments, but by some sort of vibration that renders everything at once alive and in place. Don Juan explained that those sorcerers, by means of their practices and their discipline, became capable of handling that vibratory force once they were fully conscious of it. Their expertise in dealing with it became so extraordinary that their actions were transformed into legends, mythological events that existed only as fables. For instance, one of the stories that don Juan told about the ancient sorcerers was that they were capable of dissolving their physical mass by merely placing their full consciousness and *intent* on that force.

Don Juan stated that, although they were capable of actually going through a pinhole if they deemed it necessary, they were never quite satisfied with the result of this maneuver of dissolving their mass. The reason for their discontent was that once their mass was dissolved, their capacity to act vanished. They were left with the alternative of only witnessing events in which they were incapable of participating. Their ensuing frustration, the result of being incapacitated to act, turned, according to don Juan, into their damning flaw: their obsession with uncovering the nature of that vibratory force, an obsession driven by their concreteness, which made them want to hold and control that force. Their fervent desire was to strike from the ghostlike condition of masslessness, something which don Juan said could not ever be accomplished.

Modern-day practitioners, cultural heirs of those sorcerers of antiquity, having found out that it is not possible to be concrete and utilitarian about that vibratory force, have opted for the only rational alternative: to become conscious of that force with no other purpose in sight except the elegance and well-being brought about by knowledge.

"The only permissible time," don Juan said to me once, "when modern-day sorcerers use the power of this vibratory agglutinating force, is when they burn from within, when the time comes for them to leave this world. It is simplicity itself for sorcerers to place their absolute and total consciousness on the binding force with the *intent* to burn, and off they go, like a puff of air."

Tensegrity

*T*ensegrity is the modern version of the magical passes of the shamans of ancient Mexico. The word *Tensegrity* is a most appropriate definition, because it is a mixture of two terms, *tension* and *integrity:* terms which connote the two driving forces of the magical passes. The activity created by contracting and relaxing the tendons and muscles of the body is *tension*. *Integrity* is the act of regarding the body as a sound, complete, perfect unit.

Tensegrity is taught as a system of movements, because that is the only manner in which the mysterious and vast subject of the magical passes could be faced in a modern setting. The people who now practice Tensegrity are not shaman practitioners in search of shamanistic alternatives that involve rigorous discipline, exertion, and hardships. Therefore, the emphasis of the magical passes has to be on their value as movements, and all the consequences that such movements bring forth.

Don Juan Matus had explained that the first drive of the sorcerers of his lineage who lived in Mexico in ancient times, in relation to the magical passes, was to *saturate* themselves with movement. They arranged every posture, every movement of the body that they could remember, into groups. They believed that the longer the group, the greater its effect of *saturation*, and the greater the need for the practitioners to use their memory to recall it.

The shamans of don Juan's lineage, after arranging the magical passes into long groups and practicing them as sequences, deemed that this criterion of *saturation* had fulfilled its purposes, and they dropped it. From then on, what was sought was the opposite: the fragmentation of the long groups into single segments, which were practiced as individual, independent units. The manner in which don Juan Matus taught the magical passes to his four disciples—Taisha Abelar, Florinda Donner-Grau, Carol Tiggs, and myself—was the product of this drive for fragmentation.

Don Juan's personal opinion was that the benefit of practicing the long groups was patently obvious; such practice forced the shaman initiates to use their kinesthetic memory. He considered the use of kinesthetic memory to be a real bonus, which those shamans had stumbled upon accidentally, and which had the marvelous effect of shutting off the noise of the mind: the *internal dialogue*.

Don Juan had explained to me that the way in which we reinforce our perception of the world and keep it fixed at a certain level of efficiency and function is by talking to ourselves.

"The entire human race," he said to me on one occasion, "keeps a determined level of function and efficiency by means of the *internal dialogue*. The *internal dialogue* is the key to maintaining the *assemblage point* stationary at the position shared by the entire human race: at the height of the shoulder blades, an arm's length away from them.

"By accomplishing the opposite of the *internal dialogue*," he went on, "that is to say *inner silence*, practitioners can break the fixation of their *assemblage points*, thus acquiring an extraordinary fluidity of perception."

The practice of Tensegrity has been arranged around the performance of the long groups, which in Tensegrity have been renamed *series* to avoid the generic implication of calling them just *groups*, as don Juan called them. In order to accomplish this arrangement, it was necessary to reestablish the criteria of *saturation* which had prompted the creation of the long groups. It took the practitioners of Tensegrity years of meticulous and concentrated work to reassemble a great number of the dismembered groups.

Reestablishing the criteria of *saturation* by performing the long series gave, as a result, something which don Juan had already defined as the modern goal of the magical passes: the *redeployment of energy*. Don Juan was convinced that this had always been the unspoken goal of the magical passes, even at the time of the old sorcerers. The old sorcerers didn't seem to have known this, but even if they did, they never conceptualized it in those terms. By all indications, what the old sorcerers sought avidly and experienced as a sensation of well-being and plenitude when they performed the magical passes was, in essence, the effect of unused energy being reclaimed by the centers of vitality in the body.

In Tensegrity, the long groups have been reassembled, and a great number of the fragments have been kept as single, functioning units. These units have been strung together by purpose—for instance, the purpose of *intending*, or the purpose of *recapitulation*, or the purpose of *inner silence*, and so on—creating in this fashion the Tensegrity series. In this manner, a system has been achieved in which the best results are obtained by performing long sequences of movements that definitely tax the kinesthetic memory of the practitioners.

In every other respect, the way Tensegrity is taught is a faithful reproduction of the way in which don Juan taught the magical passes to his disciples. He inundated them with a profusion of detail and let their minds be bewildered by the number and variety of magical passes taught to them, and by the implication that each of them individually was a pathway to *infinity*.

His disciples spent years overwhelmed, confused, and above all despondent, because they felt that being inundated in such a manner was an unfair onslaught on them.

"When I teach you the magical passes," he explained to me once when I questioned him about the subject, "I am following the traditional sorcerers' device of *clouding* your linear view. By *saturating* your kinesthetic memory, I am creating a pathway for you to *inner silence*.

"Since all of us," he continued, "are filled to the brim with the doings and undoings of the world of everyday life, we have very little room for kinesthetic memory. You may have noticed that you have none. When you want to imitate my movements, you cannot remain facing me. You have to stand side by side with me in order to establish in your own body what's right and what's left. Now, if a long sequence of movements were presented to you, it would take you weeks of repetition to remember all the movements. While you're trying to memorize the movements, you have to make room for them in your memory by pushing other things out of the way. That was the effect that the old sorcerers sought."

Don Juan's contention was that if his disciples kept on doggedly practicing the magical passes, in spite of their confusion, they would arrive
at a threshold when their *redeployed energy* would tip the scales, and
they would be able to handle the magical passes with absolute clarity.

When don Juan made those statements, I could hardly believe them.
Nevertheless, at one moment, just as he had said, I ceased to be confused and despondent. In a most mysterious way, the magical passes,
since they are magical, arranged themselves into extraordinary
sequences that cleared up everything. Don Juan explained that the clarity I was experiencing was the result of the *redeployment* of my energy.

The concern of people practicing Tensegrity nowadays matches
exactly my concern and the concern of don Juan's other disciples when
we first began to perform the magical passes. They feel bewildered by
the number of movements. I reiterate to them what don Juan reiterated
to me over and over: that what is of supreme importance is to practice
whatever Tensegrity sequence is remembered. The *saturation* that has
been carried on will give, in the end, the results sought by the shamans
of ancient Mexico: the *redeployment of energy*, and its three concomi-
tants—the shutting off of the *internal dialogue*, the possibility for *inner
silence*, and the fluidity of the *assemblage point*.

As a personal assessment, I can say that by *saturating* me with the
magical passes, don Juan accomplished two formidable feats: One, he
brought to the surface a flock of hidden resources that I had but didn't
know existed, such as the ability to concentrate and the ability to
remember detail; and two, he gently broke my obsession with my linear
mode of interpretation.

"What is happening to you," don Juan explained to me when I questioned him about what I was experiencing in this respect, "is that you
are feeling the advent of *inner silence*, once your *internal dialogue* has
been minimally offset. A new flux of things has begun to enter into your
field of perception. These things were always there, on the periphery of
your general awareness, but you never had enough energy to be deliberately conscious of them. As you chase away your *internal dialogue*, other
items of awareness begin to fill in the empty space, so to speak.

"The new flux of energy," he went on, "which the magical passes
have brought to your centers of vitality is making your *assemblage point*
more fluid. It's no longer rigidly palisaded. You're no longer driven by
our ancestral fears, which make us incapable of taking a step in any

direction. Sorcerers say that energy makes us free, and that is the absolute truth."

The ideal state of Tensegrity practitioners, in relation to the Tensegrity movements, is the same as the ideal state of a practitioner of shamanism in relation to the execution of the magical passes. Both are being led by the movements themselves into an unprecedented culmination. From there, the practitioners of Tensegrity will be able to execute, by themselves, for whatever effect they see fit, without any coaching from outside sources, any movement from the bulk of movements with which they have been *saturated*; they will be able to execute them with precision and speed, as they walk, or eat, or rest, or do anything, because they will have the energy to do so.

The execution of the magical passes, as shown in Tensegrity, doesn't necessarily require a particular space or prearranged time. However, the movements should be done away from sharp currents of air. Don Juan dreaded currents of air on a perspiring body. He firmly believed that not every current of air was caused by the rising or lowering of temperature in the atmosphere, and that some currents of air were actually caused by conglomerates of consolidated energy fields moving purposefully through space.

Don Juan was convinced that such conglomerates of energy fields possessed a specific type of awareness, particularly deleterious because human beings cannot ordinarily detect them, and become exposed to them indiscriminately. The deleterious effect of such conglomerates of energy fields is especially prevalent in a large metropolis, where they could be easily disguised as, if nothing else, the momentum created by the speed of passing automobiles.

Something else to bear in mind when practicing Tensegrity is that since the goal of the magical passes is something foreign to Western man, an effort should be made to keep the practice of Tensegrity detached from the concerns of our daily world. The practice of Tensegrity should not be mixed with elements with which we are already thoroughly familiar, such as conversation, music, or the sound of a radio or TV newsman reporting the news, no matter how muffled the sound might be.

The setting of modern urban life facilitates the formation of groups, and under these circumstances, the only manner in which Tensegrity can be taught and practiced in the seminars and workshops is in groups of practitioners. Practicing in groups is beneficial in many aspects and deleterious in others. It is beneficial because it allows the creation of a consensus of movement and the opportunity to learn by examination and comparison. It is deleterious because it fosters the reliance on others, and the emergence of syntactic commands and solicitations dealing with hierarchy.

Don Juan conceived that since the totality of human behavior was ruled by language, human beings have learned to respond to what he called *syntactic commands*, praising or deprecatory formulas built into language—for example, the responses that each individual makes, or elicits in others, with slogans such as *No problem, Piece of cake, It's time to worry, You could do better, I can't do it, My butt is too big, I'm the best, I'm the worst in the world, I could live with that, I'm coping, Everything's going to be okay*, etc., etc. Don Juan maintained that what sorcerers have always wanted, as a basic rule of thumb, is to run away from activities derived from syntactic commands.

Originally, as don Juan described it, the magical passes were performed by the shamans of ancient Mexico individually and in solitariness, on the spur of the moment or as the necessity arose. He taught them to his disciples in the same fashion. Don Juan stated that for the shaman practitioners, the challenge of performing the magical passes has always been to execute them perfectly, holding in mind only the abstract view of their perfect execution. Ideally, Tensegrity should be taught and practiced in the same fashion. However, the conditions of modern life and the fact that the goal of the magical passes has been formulated to apply to a great number of people make it imperative that a new approach be taken. Tensegrity should be practiced in whatever form is easiest: either in groups, or alone, or both.

In my particular case, the practice of Tensegrity in very large groups has been more than ideal, because it has given me the unique opportunity of witnessing something which don Juan Matus and all the sorcerers of his lineage never did: the effects of *human mass*. Don Juan and all the shamans of his lineage, which he considered to be twenty-seven generations long, never were capable of witnessing the effects of human mass. They practiced the magical passes alone, or in groups of up to five practitioners. For them, the magical passes were highly individualistic.

If the number of Tensegrity practitioners is in the hundreds, an energetic current is nearly instantaneously formed among them. This ener-

getic current, which a shaman could easily *see*, creates in the practitioners a sense of urgency. It is like a vibratory wind that sweeps through
them, and gives them the primary elements of purpose. I have been
privileged to *see* something I considered to be a portentous sight: the
awakening of purpose, the energetic basis of man. Don Juan Matus used
to call this *unbending intent*. He taught me that *unbending intent* is the
essential tool of those who journeyed into the unknown.

A very important issue to consider when practicing Tensegrity is that
the movements must be executed with the idea that the benefit of the
magical passes comes by itself. This idea must be stressed at any cost. At
the beginning, it is very difficult to discern the fact that Tensegrity is not a
standard system of movements for developing the body. It indeed develops
the body, but only as a by-product of a more transcendental effect. By *redeploying* unused energy, the magical passes can conduce the practitioner to
a level of awareness in which the parameters of normal, traditional perception are canceled out by the fact that they are expanded. The practitioner can thus be allowed even to enter into unimaginable worlds.

"But why would I want to enter into those worlds?" I asked don Juan
when he described this post-effect of the magical passes.

"Because you are a creature of awareness, a perceiver, like the rest of
us," he said. "Human beings are on a journey of awareness, which has
been momentarily interrupted by extraneous forces. Believe me, we are
magical creatures of awareness. If we don't have this conviction, we
have nothing."

He further explained that human beings, from the moment their *journey of awareness* was interrupted, have been caught in an eddy, so to
speak, and are spinning around, having the impression of moving with
the current, and yet remaining stationary.

"Take my word," don Juan went on, "because mine are not arbitrary
statements. My word is the result of corroborating, for myself, what the
shamans of ancient Mexico found out: that we human beings are magical beings."

It has taken me thirty years of hard discipline to come to a cognitive
plateau in which don Juan's statements are recognizable and their valid-
ity is established beyond the shadow of a doubt. I know now that human
beings are creatures of awareness, involved in an evolutionary *journey of
awareness*, beings indeed unknown to themselves, filled to the brim
with incredible resources that are never used.

Six Series of Tensegrity

The six series which are going to be discussed are the following:

1. The Series for Preparing *Intent*
2. The Series for the Womb
3. The Series of the Five Concerns: The Westwood Series
4. The Separation of the Left Body and the Right Body: The Heat Series
5. The Masculinity Series
6. The Series for Devices Used in Conjunction with Specific Magical Passes

The particular magical passes of Tensegrity that comprise each of the six series conform with a criterion of maximum efficiency. In other words, each magical pass is a precise ingredient of a formula. This is a replica of the way in which the long series of magical passes were originally used; each series was sufficient in itself to produce the maximum release of *redeployable energy*.

In executing the magical passes, there are certain things that must be taken into consideration in order to perform the movements with maximum efficiency:

1. All the magical passes of the six series can be repeated as many times as desired, unless otherwise specified. If they are first done with the left side of the body, they must be repeated an equal number of times with the right side. As a rule, every magical pass of the six series begins with the left side.

2. The feet are kept separate by a distance equivalent to the shoulders' width. This is a balanced way to distribute the weight of the body. If the legs are spread too far apart, the balance of the body is impaired. The same thing happens if they are too close together. The best way to arrive at this distance is to begin from a position where the two feet are close together (fig. 1). The tips of the feet are then pivoted on the fixed heels and opened in a letter V shape (fig. 2). Shifting the weight to the tips of the feet, the heels are pivoted out to the sides an equal distance (fig. 3). The tips of the feet are brought into parallel alignment, and the distance between the feet is roughly the width of the shoulders. Further adjustment may be necessary here in order to reach that desired width and to get the optimal balance of the body.

Figure 1   Figure 2   Figure 3

3. During the execution of all the magical passes of Tensegrity, the knees are kept slightly bent, so that when one is looking down, the kneecaps block the view of the tips of the feet (figs. 4, 5), except in the case of specific magical passes in which the knees have to be locked. Such cases are indicated in the description of those passes. To have the knees locked doesn't mean that the hamstrings are injuriously tense, but rather that they are locked in a gentle way, without unnecessary force.

This position of bending the knees is a modern addition to the execution of the magical passes, one that stems from influences of recent times. One of the leaders of don Juan Matus's lineage was the *nagual* Lujan, a sailor from China whose original name was something like Lo-

Figure 4   Figure 5

Ban. He came to Mexico around the turn of the nineteenth century, and stayed there for the rest of his life. One of the women sorcerers in don Juan Matus's own party went to the Orient and studied martial arts. Don Juan Matus himself recommended that his disciples learn to move in a disciplined fashion by taking up some form of martial arts training.

Another issue to consider in reference to the slightly bent knees is that when the legs are moved forward in a kicking motion, the knees are never whipped. Rather, the whole leg should be moved by the tension of the muscles of the thighs. Moving in this fashion, the tendons of the knees are never injured.

4. The back muscles of the legs must be tensed (fig. 6). This is a very difficult accomplishment. Most people can learn quite easily to tense the front muscles of the legs, but the back muscles of the legs still remain flaccid. Don Juan said that the back muscles of the thighs are where personal history is always stored in the body. According to him, feelings find their home there and get stagnant. He maintained that difficulty in changing behavior patterns could be easily attributed to the flaccidity of the back muscles of the thighs.

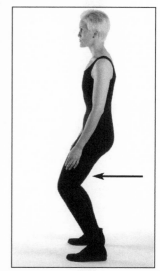

Figure 6

5. While performing all these magical passes, the arms are always kept slightly bent at the elbows—never fully extended—when they are moved to strike, preventing, in this manner, the tendons of the elbows from becoming irritated (fig. 7).

6. The thumb must always be kept in a *locked* position, meaning that it is folded over the edge of the hand. It should never stick out (fig. 8). The sorcerers of don Juan's lineage considered the thumb to be a crucial element in terms of energy and function. They believed that at the base of the thumb exist points where energy can become stagnant, and points that can regulate the flow of energy in the body. In order to avoid unnecessary stress on the thumb or injury resulting from jolting the hand forcefully, they adopted the measure of pressing the thumbs against the inside edges of the hands.

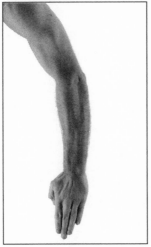 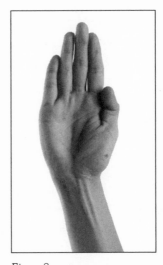

Figure 7   Figure 8

7. When the hand is made into a fist, the little finger is raised to avoid an angular fist (fig. 9) in which the middle, fourth, and fifth fingers droop. The idea is that in making a square fist (fig. 10), the fourth and fifth fingers have to be raised, thus creating a peculiar tension in the axilla, a tension which is most desirable for general well-being.

8. The hands, when they have to be opened, are fully extended. The tendons of the back of the hand are at work, presenting the palm as an even, flat surface (fig. 11). Don Juan preferred a flat palm to counteract the tendency (established, he felt, through socialization) to present the

Figure 9

Figure 10

hand as a hollow palm (fig. 12). He said that a hollow palm was the palm of a beggar, and that whoever practices the magical passes is a warrior, not a beggar in the least.

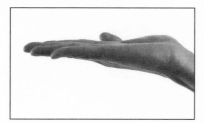

Figure 11   Figure 12

9. When the fingers have to be contracted at the second knuckle and bent tightly over the palm, the tendons on the back of the hand are tensed to the maximum, especially the tendons of the thumb (fig. 13). This tension of the tendons creates a pressure on the wrists and forearms, areas which sorcerers of ancient Mexico believed were key in promoting health and well-being.

10. In many Tensegrity movements, the wrists have to be bent forward or backward to an approximately ninety-degree angle by contracting the tendons of the forearm (fig. 14). This bending must be accomplished slowly, because most of the time the wrist is quite inflexible, and it is important that the wrist acquire the flexibility to turn the back of the hand to make a maximum angle with the forearm.

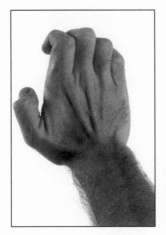

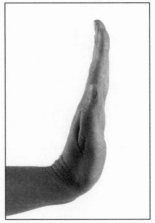

Figure 13   Figure 14

11. Another important issue in the practice of Tensegrity is an act which has been termed *turning the body on*. This is a unique act in which all the muscles of the body, and specifically the diaphragm, are contracted in one instant. The muscles of the stomach and abdomen are jolted, as are the muscles around the shoulders and shoulder blades. The arms and legs are tensed in unison with equal force, but only for an instant (figs. 15, 16). As practitioners of Tensegrity progress in their practice, they can learn to sustain this tension for a while longer.

Turning the body on has nothing to do with the state of perennial bod-

Figure 15   Figure 16

ily tension that seems to be the mark of our times. When the body is tense with preoccupation or overwork, and the muscles of the neck are as hard as they can be, the body is not in any way turned on. Relaxing the muscles or arriving at a state of tranquillity is not turning the body off, either. The idea of the sorcerers of ancient Mexico was that with their magical passes, the body was alerted; it was made to be ready for action. Don Juan Matus termed this condition *turning the body on.* He said that when the muscular tension of *turning the body on* ceases, the body is turned off naturally.

12. Breath and breathing were, according to don Juan, of supreme importance for the sorcerers of ancient Mexico. They divided breath into breathing with the tops of the lungs, breathing with the midsection of the lungs, and breathing with the abdomen (figs. 17, 18, 19). Breathing by expanding the diaphragm they called the *animal breath,* and they practiced it assiduously, don Juan said, for longevity and health.

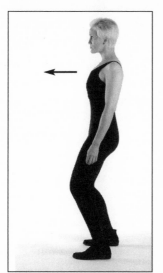  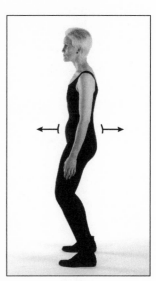

Figure 17   *Figure 18*   *Figure 19*

It was don Juan Matus's belief that many of the health problems of modern man could be easily corrected by deep breathing. He maintained that the tendency of human beings nowadays is to take shallow breaths. One of the aims of the sorcerers of ancient Mexico was to train their bodies, by means of the magical passes, to inhale and exhale deeply.

It is highly recommended, therefore, in the movements of Tensegrity that call for deep inhalations and exhalations, that these be accomplished by slowing down the inflow or outflow of air, in order to make the inhalations and exhalations longer and more profound.

Another important issue concerning the breathing in Tensegrity is that breathing is normal while executing the Tensegrity movements, unless otherwise specified in the description of any given magical pass.

13. Another consideration in performing the Tensegrity movements is the realization that has to come to practitioners that Tensegrity is in essence the interplay between relaxing and tensing the muscles of choice parts of the body in order to arrive at a most coveted physical explosion, which the sorcerers of ancient Mexico knew only as the *energy of the tendons*. This is a veritable explosion of the nerves and tendons below or at the core of the muscles.

Given that Tensegrity is the tension and relaxation of muscles, the intensity of the muscle tension and the length of time that the muscles are kept in that state, in any given magical pass, depends on the strength of the participant. It is recommended that at the beginning of the practice, the tension be minimal and the length of time as brief as possible. As the body gets warmer, the tension should become greater and the length of time extended, but always in a moderate fashion.

The Series for Preparing Intent

Don Juan Matus stated that human beings as organisms perform a stupendous maneuver of perception which, unfortunately, creates a misconception, a false front; they take the influx of sheer energy in the universe at large and turn it into sensory data, which they interpret according to a strict system of interpretation that sorcerers call *the human form*. This magical act of interpreting pure energy gives rise to the misconception, the peculiar conviction of human beings that their interpretation system is all that exists.

Don Juan elucidated this phenomenon with an example. He said that *tree*, as *tree* is known to human beings, is more interpretation than perception. He pointed out that for human beings to establish the presence of *tree*, all they need is a cursory glance that tells them hardly anything. The rest is a phenomenon which he described as the *calling of intent*, the *intent of tree*; that is to say, the interpretation of sensory data pertaining to the specific phenomenon that human beings call *tree*. He declared that the entire world of human beings, just as in this example, is composed of an endless repertoire of interpretations where human senses play a minimal role. In other words, only the visual sense touches the energy influx which comes from the universe at large, and it does so only in a cursory fashion.

He maintained that the majority of the perceptual activity of human beings is interpretation, and that human beings are the kind of organisms that need only a minimal input of pure perception in order to create their world; or, that they perceive only enough to trigger their interpretation system. The example that don Juan liked the best was the way in which he said we construct, by *intending*, something as overwhelming and as crucial as the White House. He called the White House the site of power of today's world, the center of all our endeavors, hopes, fears, and so on, as a global conglomerate of human beings—for all practical purposes, the capital of the civilized world. He said that all this wasn't in the realm of the abstract, or even in the realm of our minds, but in the realm of *intending*, because from the point of view of our sensory input, the White House was a building that in no way had the richness, the scope, the depth of the concept of the White House. He added that from the point of view of the input of sensory data, the White House, like everything else in our world, was cursorily apprehended with our visual senses only; our tactile, olfactory, auditory, and taste senses were not engaged in any way. The interpretation that those senses could make of sensory data in relation to the building where the White House is would have no meaning whatsoever.

The question that don Juan asked as a sorcerer was where the White House was. He said, answering his own question, that it was certainly not in our perception, not even in our thoughts, but in a special realm of *intending*, where it was nurtured with everything pertinent to it. Don Juan's assertion was that to create a total universe of *intending* in such a manner was our magic.

Since the theme of the first series of Tensegrity is preparing the practitioners for *intending*, it's important to review the sorcerers' definition of *intending*. For don Juan, *intending* was the tacit act of filling out the empty spaces left by direct sensory perception, or the act of enriching the observable phenomena by means of *intending* a completeness that doesn't exist from the point of view of pure perception.

The act of *intending* this completeness was referred to by don Juan as *calling intent*. Everything he explained about *intent* pointed to the fact that the act of *intending* is not in the realm of the physical. In other words, it is not part of the physicality of the brain or any other organ. *Intent*, for don Juan, transcended the world we know. It is something like an energetic wave, a beam of energy which attaches itself to us.

Because of the extrinsic nature of *intent*, don Juan made a distinction between the body as part of the cognition of everyday life and the body as an energetic unit which was not part of that cognition. This energetic unit included the unseen parts of the body, such as the internal organs, and the energy that flowed through them. Don Juan asserted that it was with this part that energy could be directly perceived.

He pointed out that because of the predominance of sight in our habitual way of perceiving the world, the shamans of ancient Mexico described the act of directly apprehending energy as *seeing*. For them to perceive energy as it flowed in the universe meant that energy adopted nonidiosyncratic, specific configurations that repeated themselves consistently, and that those configurations could be perceived in the same terms by anyone who *saw*.

The most important example don Juan Matus could give of this consistency of energy in adopting specific configurations was the perception of the human body when it was *seen* directly as energy. As it was already said, shamans like don Juan perceive a human being as a conglomerate of energy fields that gives the total impression of a clear-cut sphere of luminosity. Taken in this sense, energy is described by shamans as a vibration that agglutinates itself into cohesive units. Shamans describe the entire universe as being composed of energy configurations that appear to the *seeing* eye as filaments, or luminous fibers that are strung in every which way without ever being entangled. This is an incomprehensible proposition for the linear mind. It has a built-in contradiction that can't be resolved: How could those fibers extend themselves every which way and yet not be entangled?

Don Juan emphasized the point that shamans were able only to describe events, and that if their terms of description seemed inadequate and contradictory, it was because of the limitations of syntax. Yet their descriptions were as strict as anything could be.

The shamans of ancient Mexico, according to don Juan, described *intent* as a perennial force that permeates the entire universe—a force that is aware of itself to the point of responding to the beckoning or to the command of shamans. By means of *intent*, those shamans were capable of unleashing not only all the human possibilities of perceiving, but all the human possibilities of action. Through *intent*, they realized the most far-fetched formulations.

Don Juan taught me that the limit of man's capability of perceiving is called the *band of man*, meaning that there is a boundary that marks human capabilities as dictated by the human organism. These boundaries are not merely the traditional boundaries of orderly thought, but the boundaries of the totality of resources locked within the human organism. Don Juan believed that these resources are never used, but are kept in situ by preconceived ideas about human limitations, limitations that have nothing to do with actual human potential.

Don Juan stated, as categorically as he was able to, that since perceiving energy as it flows in the universe is not arbitrary or idiosyncratic, seers witness formulations of energy that happen by themselves and are not molded by human interference. Thus, the perception of such formulations is, in itself and by itself, the key that releases the locked-in human potential that ordinarily has never entered into play. In order to elicit the perception of those energetic formulations, the totality of human capabilities to perceive has to be engaged.

The Series for Preparing *Intent* is divided into four groups. The first is called Mashing Energy for *Intent*. The second is called Stirring Up Energy for *Intent*. The third group is called Gathering Energy for *Intent*, and the fourth group is called Breathing In the Energy of *Intent*.

The First Group:
Mashing Energy for *Intent*

Don Juan gave me explanations which covered all the nuances of every group of magical passes, which are the core of the long Tensegrity Series.

"Energy which is essential for handling *intent*," he said when he was explaining to me the energetic implications of this group, "is continuously dispelled from the vital centers located around the liver, pancreas, and kidneys, and settles down at the bottom of the luminous sphere that we are. This energy needs to be constantly stirred and rerouted. The sorcerers of my lineage were very emphatic in recommending a systematic and controlled stirring of energy with the legs and feet. For them, long walks, which were an unavoidable feature of their lives, resulted in an excessive stirring of energy which did not serve any purpose. Long walks were their nemesis for this reason, and the inflow of excessive energy had to be balanced by the execution of specific magical passes performed while they were walking."

Don Juan Matus told me that this set, which consists of fifteen magical passes whose function is to stir energy with the feet and legs, was considered by the shamans of his lineage to be the most effective way of doing what they called *mashing energy*. He stated that each of the steps is a magical pass which has a built-in control for the *mash-*

ing of energy, and that practitioners can repeat these magical passes hundreds of times, if they so desire, without worrying about an excessive stirring of energy. In don Juan's view, energy for *intending* that was stirred up excessively ended up further depleting the centers of vitality.

1. Grinding Energy with the Feet

The body pivots on the balls of the feet from left to right and right to left in unison for a moment in order to gain balance. Then the weight of the body is shifted to the heels, and the pivoting is done on them from then on, with the toes slightly off the ground while swiveling, and touching the ground when the feet reach the maximum slant.

The arms are kept bent at the elbows with the hands pointing out, palms facing each other. The arms move with an impulse from the shoulders and the shoulder blades. This movement of the arms in unison with the legs, as in walking (the right arm moves when the left leg moves, and vice versa), accounts for a total engagement of the limbs and the internal organs (figs. 20, 21).

Figure 20   Figure 21

A physical by-product of grinding energy in this fashion is an increase in circulation in the feet, calves, and thighs up to the groin area. Shamans throughout the centuries have also used it to restore flexibility to limbs that were injured in daily use.

2. Grinding Energy with Three Slides of the Feet

The feet are swiveled on the heels, in the same manner as in the previous magical pass, three times. There is a pause that lasts an instant and then they are swiveled three times again. It is important to notice that in all the first three magical passes of this series, the key issue is the engagement of the arms, which move back and forth briskly.

Making the grinding of energy a discontinuous affair increases its effect. A physical by-product of this magical pass is a quick surge of energy for instances of running or fleeing danger, or for anything that requires a quick intervention.

3. Grinding Energy by a Sideways Slide of the Feet

Both feet, pivoting on the heels, move to the left; they pivot on the balls of the feet to the left again. Next, they pivot a third time, still to the left, but on the heels again (figs. 22, 23, 24). The sequence is reversed by pivoting on the heels to the right; next, on the balls of the feet to the right; and then on the heels again, to the right.

Figure 22   Figure 23   Figure 24

A physical consequence of these three magical passes is the spurring of the circulation in the total body.

4. Mixing Energy by Striking the Floor with the Heels

This magical pass resembles walking in place. The knee moves up briskly while the tip of the foot rests on the ground. The weight of the body is carried by the other leg. The body weight shifts back and forth, resting on whichever leg stays put, while the other one performs the movement. The arms are moved in the same fashion as in the previous magical pass (fig. 25).

A physical consequence of this magical pass and the following one is very much like that of the three preceding magical passes: a sensation of well-being that permeates the pelvic region after performing the movements.

Figure 25

5. Mixing Energy by Striking the Ground with the Heels Three Times

This magical pass is exactly like the preceding one, with the exception that the movement of the knees and feet is not continuous. It is interrupted after the heels are brought to the ground three times, in an alternating fashion. The sequence is left, right, left—pause—right, left, right, and so on.

The first five magical passes of this group allow practitioners a quick surge of energy, in cases when energy is needed in the midsection or the groin, or, for instance, when they need to perform a long-distance run or a quick climbing of rocks or trees.

6. Gathering Energy with the Soles of the Feet and Moving It Up the Inner Legs

The soles of the left and the right foot move alternately up the inner part of the opposite leg, almost brushing it. It is important to arch the legs a little bit by standing with the knees bent (fig. 26).

In this magical pass, energy for *intending* is forced up the inner side of the legs, which shamans consider to be the storage place of kinesthetic memory. This magical pass is used as an aid to release the memory of movements, or to facilitate retaining the memory of new ones.

Figure 26

7. Stirring Energy with the Knees

The knee of the left leg is bent and swung to the right as far as it can reach, as if to give a sideways kick with the knee, while the trunk and the arms are gently twisted as far as possible in the opposite direction (fig. 27). The left leg is then brought back to a standing position. The same movement is performed with the right knee, alternating then back and forth.

Figure 27

8. Pushing the Energy Stirred with the Knees into the Trunk

This magical pass is the energetic continuation of the preceding one. The left knee, bent to the maximum, is pushed up as far as possible into the trunk. The trunk is bent slightly forward. At the moment the knee is pushed up, the tip of the foot points to the ground (fig. 28). The same movement is performed with the right leg, alternating then between the two legs.

Figure 28

Pointing the foot to the ground ensures that the tendons of the ankles are tense, in order to jolt minute centers there where energy accumulates. Shamans consider those centers to be perhaps the most important in the lower limbs, so important that they could awaken the rest of the minute energy centers in the body through the performance of this magical pass. This magical pass and the preceding one are executed together for the purpose of projecting the energy for *intending* gathered with the knees up into the two centers of vitality around the liver and the pancreas.

9. Kicking Energy in Front and in Back of the Body

A front kick of the left leg is followed by a hook kick to the back with the right leg (figs. 29, 30). Then the order is reversed and a front kick is made with the right leg, followed by a hook kick to the back with the left leg.

The arms are kept to the sides, because this magical pass engages only the lower limbs, giving them flexibility. The aim is to lift the leg that kicks to the front as high as possible, and the leg that kicks to the back also as high as possible. When executing the back kick, the trunk should bend slightly forward to facilitate the movement. This slight bending forward of the trunk is used as a natural means of absorbing the energy stirred with the limbs. This magical pass is performed to aid the body when problems of digestion arise, due to a change in diet, or when there is a need to travel over great distances.

Figure 29   *Figure 30*

10. Lifting Energy from the Soles of the Feet

The left knee is bent acutely as it is lifted toward the trunk, as far up as possible. The trunk is bent slightly forward, almost touching the knee. The arms jut down, making a vise that grabs the sole of the foot (fig. 31). The ideal would be to grab the sole of the foot in a very light fashion, releasing it immediately. The foot comes down to the ground as the arms and hands, with a powerful jolt that engages the shoulders and pectoral muscles, lift up along the sides of the legs to the level of the pancreas and spleen (fig. 32). The same movements are performed with the right foot and arm, lifting the hands from the feet to the level of the liver and gallbladder. The movements are performed alternating between the two legs.

Figure 31   Figure 32

As in the case of the previous magical pass, bending the trunk forward allows the energy from the soles of the feet to be transferred to the two vital centers of energy around the liver and the pancreas. This magical pass is used to aid the attainment of flexibility, and to relieve problems of digestion.

11. Pushing Down a Wall of Energy

The left foot, with the knee acutely bent, is lifted to the height of the hips; then it pushes forward with the tip of the foot arched upward, as if pushing away a solid object (fig. 33). As soon as the foot is brought down, the right foot is lifted in the same fashion and the movement is repeated, alternating the feet.

Figure 33

12. Stepping Over a Barrier of Energy
The left leg is nimbly lifted as if going over a hurdle which is located edgewise in front of the body. The leg makes a circle from left to right (fig. 34), and once the foot lands, the other leg is lifted to perform the same movement.

Figure 34

13. Kicking a Lateral Gate

This is a kick-push with the soles of the feet. The left leg is lifted to midcalf and the foot pushes to the right of the body as if to hit a solid object, using the total sole of the foot as a striking surface (fig. 35). The foot is retrieved then to the left side, and the same movement is repeated with the right leg and foot.

Figure 35

14. Cracking a Nugget of Energy

The left foot is lifted with the tip pointing acutely to the ground. The knee protrudes straight forward, deeply bent. Then the foot descends with a controlled motion, striking toward the ground as if it were cracking a nugget (fig. 36). Once the tip of the foot strikes, the foot is returned to its original standing position and the same movement is repeated with the other leg and foot.

15. Scraping Off the Mud of Energy

The left foot is lifted a few inches above the ground; the entire leg is brought forward and then pushed backward sharply, with the foot lightly brushing the ground as if it were scraping something off the sole of the foot (fig. 37). The weight of the body is carried by the opposite leg, and the trunk leans a bit forward in order to engage the muscles of the stomach as this magical pass is executed. Once the left foot returns to its normal position, the same movement is repeated with the right foot and leg.

* * *

Shamans call the last five magical passes of this group *Steps in Nature*. They are magical passes that practitioners can perform as they walk, or conduct business, or even as they are sitting, talking to people. Their function is gathering energy with the feet and using it with the legs for situations in which concentration and the quick use of memory are required.

Figure 36   *Figure 37*

The Second Group:
Stirring Up Energy for *Intent*

The ten magical passes of the second group have to do with stirring up energy for *intending* from areas just below the knees, above the head, around the kidneys, the liver and pancreas, the solar plexus, and the neck. Each of these magical passes is a tool that stirs up exclusively the energy pertinent to *intending*, which is accumulated on those areas. Shamans consider these magical passes to be essential for daily living, because for them, life is ruled by *intent*. This set of magical passes is perhaps for shamans what a cup of coffee is for modern man. The slogan of our day, "I'm not myself until I drink my cappuccino," or the slogan of a past generation, "I'm not awake until I drink my cup of java," is rendered for them as "I am not ready for anything until I have performed these magical passes." The second group of this series begins by the act that has been termed *turning the body on*. (See page 34, figs. 15, 16.)

16. Stirring Up Energy with the Feet and the Arms

After the body has been *turned on*, it is held in a slightly stooped-over position (fig. 38). The weight is placed on the right leg while the left leg makes a complete circle, brushing the ground with the tips of the toes, and landing on the ball of the foot, in front of the body. The left arm, in synchronization with the leg, makes a circle, the top of which goes above the level of the head (fig. 39). There is a slight pause of the leg and arm and they draw two more circles in succession, making a total of three (fig. 40). The rhythm of this magical pass is given by counting one, slight pause, one-one, then a very slight pause, two, pause, two-two, then a very slight pause, and so on. The same movement is performed with the right leg and arm.

This magical pass stirs energy at the bottom of the *luminous ball* with the feet, and projects it with the arms to the area just above the head.

Figure 38   Figure 39   Figure 40

17. Rolling Energy on the Adrenals

The forearms are placed behind the body, over the area of the kidneys and adrenals. The elbows are bent at a ninety-degree angle and the hands are held in fists, a few inches away from the body, without touching it. The fists move downward in a rotational fashion, one on top of the other, beginning with the left fist moving downward; the right fist follows, moving downward as the left fist moves back up. The trunk leans slightly forward (fig. 41). Then the movement is reversed, and the fists roll in the opposite direction as the trunk leans slightly backward (fig. 42). Leaning the body forward and backward in this fashion engages the muscles of the upper arms and the shoulders.

This magical pass is used to supply the energy of *intending* to the adrenals and kidneys.

Figure 41   Figure 42

18. Stirring up Energy for the Adrenals

The trunk is bent forward, with the knees protruding beyond the line of the toes. The hands rest above the kneecaps, the fingers draping over them. The left hand then rotates to the right over the kneecap, making the elbow protrude as far forward as possible in alignment with the left

knee (fig. 43). At the same time, the right forearm, with the hand still above the kneecap, rests its full length over the right thigh, while the right knee is straightened out, engaging the hamstring. It is important to move only the knees, and not to swing the rear end from side to side.

Figure 43   Figure 44

The same movements are performed with the right arm and leg (fig. 44).

This magical pass is employed for stirring up the energy of *intending* around the kidneys and adrenals. It brings the practitioner long-range endurance and a sensation of daring and self-confidence.

19. Fusing Left and Right Energy

A deep inhalation is taken. A very slow exhalation begins as the left forearm is brought in front of the shoulders, with the elbow bent at a ninety-degree angle. The wrist is bent backward as acutely as possible, with the fingers pointing forward, and the palm of the hand facing to the right (fig. 45).

While the arm maintains this position, the trunk is bent forward sharply until the protruding left arm reaches the level of the knees. The left elbow must be kept from sagging toward the floor, and must be maintained away from the knees, and as far forward as possible. The slow exhalation continues, as the right arm makes a full circle over the head and the right hand comes to rest an inch or two away from the fingers of the left hand. The palm of the right hand faces the body and the fingers point toward the floor. The head is facing downward, with the neck held straight. The exhalation ends, and a deep breath is taken in that position. All the muscles of the back and the arms and legs are contracted as the air is slowly and deeply inhaled (fig. 46).

The body straightens up as an exhalation is made, and the complete magical pass is started again with the right arm.

Figure 45   Figure 46

The maximum stretch of the arms forward permits the creation of an opening in the energetic vortex of the center of the kidneys and adrenals; such an opening allows the optimal utilization of *redeployed energy*. This magical pass is essential for the *redeployment of energy* to that center, which accounts, in general terms, for an overall vitality and youth of the body.

20. Piercing the Body with a Beam of Energy
The left arm is placed against the body in front of the navel, and the right arm just behind the body at the same level. The wrists are bent sharply, and the fingers point to the floor. The palm of the left hand faces right, and the palm of the right hand faces left (fig. 47). The fingertips of both hands are raised briskly to point in a straight line forward and backward. The whole body is tensed and the knees are bent at the instant that the fingers point forward and backward (fig. 48). The hands are kept in that position for a moment. Then the muscles are relaxed, the legs are straightened, and the arms are swiveled around until the right arm is in front and the left behind. As at the beginning of this magical pass, the fingertips point to the floor, and are raised again

Figure 47   *Figure 48*

briskly to point in a straight line forward and backward, again with a slight exhalation; the knees are bent.

By means of this magical pass, a dividing line is established in the middle of the body, which separates left energy and right energy.

21. Twisting Energy Over Two Centers of Vitality

It's a good idea to begin by placing the hands facing each other, as a device to keep the hands in line. The fingers are kept open and clawed, as if to grab the lid of a jar the size of the hand. Then the right hand is placed over the area of the pancreas and spleen, facing the body. The left hand is placed behind the body, over the area of the left kidney and adrenal, also with the palm facing the body. Both wrists are then bent backward sharply, as the trunk turns as far to the left as possible, keeping the knees in place. Next, both hands pivot at the wrists in unison, in a side-to-side movement, as if to unscrew the lids of two jars, one on the pancreas and spleen, and the other on the left kidney (fig. 49).

The same movement is executed by reversing the order, putting the left hand in the front, at the level of the liver and gallbladder and the right arm in the back at the level of the right kidney.

With the aid of this magical pass, energy is stirred on the three main centers of vitality: the liver and gallbladder, the pancreas and spleen, and the kidneys and adrenals. It is an indispensable magical pass for those who have to be on the lookout. It facilitates an all-around awareness and it increases the practitioners' sensibility to their surroundings.

Figure 49

22. The Half-Circle of Energy

A half-circle is drawn with the left hand, commencing in front of the face. The hand moves slightly to the right until it reaches the level of the right shoulder (fig. 50). There the hand turns and draws the inner edge of a half-circle close to the left side of the body (fig. 51). The hand turns again in the back (fig. 52) and draws the outer edge of the half-circle, then returns to its initial position (fig. 53). The complete half-circle is slanted from the level of the eyes, in front, to a level below the rear end, in the back. It is important to follow the movement of the hand with the eyes.

Once the half-circle drawn with the left arm is completed, another one is drawn with the right arm, surrounding the body in this fashion with two half-circles. These two half-circles are drawn to stir energy and

4 30

Jan 18
The Tao of Physics
Fitja Capra
The Dancing Wu-
Li Masters
Gary Zugav

Figure 51   *Figure 52*   *Figure 53*

to facilitate the sliding of energy from above the head to the region of the adrenals. This magical pass is a vehicle for acquiring intense, sustained sobriety.

23. Stirring Energy Around the Neck

The left hand, with the palm facing upward, and the right hand, with the palm facing downward, are placed in front of the body, at the level of the solar plexus. The right hand is on top of the left, nearly touching it. The elbows are bent sharply. A deep breath is taken; the arms are raised slightly as the trunk is made to rotate as far to the left as possible without moving the legs, especially the knees, which are slightly bent in order to avoid any unnecessary stress on the tendons. The head is kept in alignment with the trunk and shoulders. An exhalation begins as the elbows are then gently pulled away from each other to a maximum stretch, keeping the wrists straight (fig. 54). An inhalation is taken. An exhalation begins when the head is turned very gently to the back to face the left elbow, and then to the front to face the right elbow; the rotation of the head back and forth is repeated two more times as the exhalation ends.

Figure 54

The trunk is turned to the front, and the hands reverse position there. The right hand is made to face upward while the left hand is made to face downward, on top of the right one. An inhalation is taken again. The trunk is then turned to the right, and the same movements are repeated on the right.

Shamans believe that a special type of energy for *intending* is dispersed from the *center for decisions*, located in the hollow V spot at the base of the neck, and that this energy is exclusively gathered with this magical pass.

24. Kneading Energy with a Push of the Shoulder Blades

Both arms are placed in front of the face, at the level of the eyes, with the elbows bent enough to give the arms a bowlike appearance (fig. 55). The trunk is bent forward slightly, in order to allow the shoulder blades to expand laterally. The movement begins by pushing the left arm forward while it is kept arched and tense (fig. 56). The right arm follows;

Figure 55   Figure 56

and the arms move in an alternating fashion. It is important to note that the arms are kept extremely tense. The palms of the hands face forward and the fingertips face each other. The driving force of the arms is created by the deep movement of the shoulder blades and the tenseness of the stomach muscles.

Shamans believe that energy on the ganglia around the shoulder blades gets easily stuck and becomes stagnant, bringing about the decay of the *center for decisions*, located on the V spot at the base of the neck. This magical pass is employed to stir that energy.

25. Stirring Energy Above the Head and Cracking It

The left arm moves in a relaxed fashion, making two and a half circles above and around the head (fig. 57). Those circles are then cracked with the outer edge of the forearm and the hand, which comes down forcefully, but very slowly (fig. 58). The impact is absorbed by the stomach muscles, which are tensed at that moment. The muscles of the arm are kept tight, in order to avoid injuries to the tendons which could occur if the muscles of the arm were loose, or if the arm were whipped. Air is exhaled lightly as the arm strikes downward. The same movement is repeated with the right arm.

Figure 57   Figure 58

The energy stirred and cracked in this fashion is allowed to seep downward over the entire body. When practitioners are overtired, and can't afford to go to sleep, executing this magical pass dispels sleepiness and brings forth a sensation of temporary alertness.

The Third Group:
Gathering Energy for *Intent*

The nine magical passes of the third group are employed to bring to the three centers of vitality around the liver, the pancreas, and the kidneys the specialized energy which has been stirred up by the magical passes of the previous group. The magical passes of this group must be performed slowly and with ultimate deliberation. Shamans recommend that the state of mind on executing these passes be one of total silence and the unwavering *intent* to gather the energy necessary for *intending*.

All of the magical passes of the third group begin with a fast shake of the hands, which are held at the sides of the body, with the arms hanging at a normal position. The hands shake as if the fingers were vibrating downward, taken by a tremor. A vibration of this nature was thought to be the means to stir energy around the hips and also the means to stimulate minute centers of energy where energy could get stagnant on the backs of the hands and the wrists.

The overall effect of the first three magical passes of this group is one of general vitality and well-being, since energy is carried to the three main vital centers in the lower part of the body.

26. Reaching for Energy Stirred Below the Knees
A small jump forward is made with the left leg, which is propelled by the right one. The trunk is bent markedly forward, and the left arm is stretched out to grab something that is almost at the floor level (fig. 59). The left leg is then retrieved to a standing position, and the left palm brushes immediately over the vital center of energy on the right: the liver and gallbladder.

The same movement is repeated with the right leg and arm, brushing the palm over the vital center on the left: the pancreas and spleen.

Figure 59

27. Transporting Front Energy to the Adrenals
A deep inhalation is taken while the hands shake. Then the left arm shoots straight in front of the body at the level of the shoulders with the

palm of the hand turned toward the left, as all the air is sharply exhaled (fig. 60). Next, a very slow inhalation begins while the wrist rotates from left to right, making a complete circle, as if scooping a ball of solid matter (fig. 61). Then the inhalation continues while the wrist rotates back again to its initial position with the palm facing to the left. Next, as if carrying the ball, the left arm makes a semi-circle, keeping the same shoulder level; this movement ends when the back of the bent wrist is placed over the left kidney. It is important that the continuous inhalation be made to last for the duration of the swinging of the arm from front to back. As this swinging movement is executed, the right arm makes a circular movement to the front of the body, ending when the back of the bent wrist is brought to touch the area just above the pubis. The head is turned to the left to face the back (fig. 62). Next, the left hand, which is holding the ball, turns to face the body and smashes the ball against the left kidney and adrenal. The palm is then gently rubbed over that area as an exhalation is made.

The same movement is executed by reversing the arms and turning the head to the right.

Figure 60   *Figure 61*   *Figure 62*

28. Scooping Energy from the Left and the Right

The arms are moved to the sides of the body and then raised with the hands curled inward toward the body, brushing upward against the torso to reach the armpits, as a deep inhalation is taken (fig. 63). Next, the arms are extended laterally, with the palms down, as the air is exhaled forcefully. A deep inhalation is taken then as the hands are cupped and made to rotate on the wrists until the palms face up, as if scooping something solid (fig. 64). Next, the hands are brought back to the shoulder level by bending the elbows sharply as the inhalation continues (fig. 65). This movement engages the shoulder blades and the muscles of the neck. After holding this position for a moment, the arms are extended laterally again, with a sharp exhalation. The palms face front. The palms of the hands are cupped and made to rotate backward, again as if scooping a solid substance. The slightly cupped hands are brought back to the shoulder level as before. These movements are repeated one more time, for a total of three. The palms then rub gently over the two vital centers around the liver and around the pancreas as the air is exhaled.

Figure 63   Figure 64   Figure 65

29. Cracking the Circle of Energy
A circle is made by moving the left arm to the right shoulder (fig. 66), then close around the front of the body to the back (fig. 67) and out again to in front of the face (fig. 68). This movement of the left arm is coordinated with the same movement done with the right arm. Both arms move in an alternate fashion, creating a slanted circle around the total body. Then a backward step to the left is taken with the right foot, followed by a step to the right taken with the left foot, so as to turn around to face the opposite direction.

The left arm is arched then around the left side of the circle, as if the circle were a solid object which the left arm presses against the armpit

Figure 66   *Figure 67*   *Figure 68*

and chest area. The right arm then performs the same movement on the right side, treating the circle as if it were a solid object (fig. 69). A deep breath is taken, and the circle is cracked from both sides by tensing the whole body, especially the arms, which are brought together to the chest. The palms then rub gently on the respective centers of vitality on the front of the body as the air is exhaled.

The uses of this pass are quite esoteric, because they have to do with the clarity of *intent* needed for decision making. This magical pass is used for spreading the energy of decisions accumulated around the neck.

Figure 69

30. Gathering Energy from the Front of the Body, Right Above the Head

A deep inhalation is taken as the hands shake. Both arms are brought to the level of the face with clenched fists, crossed in an X, with the left arm closer to the face, and the inside of the fisted palms toward the face. The arms are then extended a few inches to the front as the wrists are made to rotate on each other until the fisted palms are facing down (fig. 70). From this position, the left shoulder and shoulder blade are extended forward, an exhalation begins. The left shoulder is pulled back as the right one comes forward. Next, the crossed arms are lifted above the head and the exhalation ends.

A slow, deep inhalation is taken as the crossed arms make a complete circle, moving to the right around the front of the body, almost to the level of the knees, then to the left, and back to their initial position, right above the head (fig. 71). Then the arms are forcefully separated as a long exhalation begins (fig. 72). From there, the arms move as far

Figure 70   Figure 71   Figure 72

back as possible, as the exhalation continues, drawing a circle which is completed when the fists are brought to the front to the level of the eyes, with the inside of the fisted palms toward the face (fig. 73). Then the arms are crossed again. The wrists pivot on each other as the hands are opened and are placed against the body, the right hand on the area of the pancreas and spleen, and the left hand on the area of the liver and gallbladder. The body bends forward at the waist, at a ninety-degree angle, as the exhalation ends (fig. 74).

The use of this magical pass is twofold: First, it stirs energy around the shoulder blades and transports it to a place above the head. From there, it makes the energy circulate in a broad circle that touches the edges of the luminous sphere. Second, it mixes the energy of the left and the right by placing it on the two centers of vitality around the pancreas and the liver, with each hand on the opposite center.

Mixing energy in such a fashion provides a jolt of great magnitude to

Figure 73   Figure 74

the respective centers of vitality. As the practitioners became more proficient in their practice, the jolt becomes more acute, and acquires the
quality of a filter of energy, which is an incomprehensible statement
until this pass is practiced. The sensation that accompanies it could be
described as breathing mentholated air.

31. Stirring and Grabbing Energy from Below the Knees and Above the Head

An inhalation is taken as the hands shake. Both hands are brought up by
the sides of the body to the level of the waist, and held relaxed. The
knees are bent as the left hand is pushed downward with the wrist turned
so that the palm faces outward, away from the body, as if it were reaching
into a bucket full of liquid substance. This movement is performed at the
same time that the right hand shoots up above the head with equal force;
the right wrist is also turned so that the palm faces outward, away from
the body (fig. 75). A slow exhalation begins when both arms reach their
maximum extension. The wrists are returned with great force to a
straight position at the same time that the hands clasp into fists, as if
grabbing something solid. Keeping the fists clenched, the exhalation
continues while the right arm is brought down and the left arm is
brought up to the level of the waist, slowly and with great strength, as if
wading through a heavy liquid (fig. 76). Then the palms rub gently on
the areas of the liver and gallbladder and the pancreas and spleen. The

knees are straightened and the exhalation ends at this point (fig. 77).

The same movement is executed by shifting the arms; the right arm plunges downward while the left arm pushes upward.

Figure 75

Figure 76

Figure 77

The energy for *intending* that is extracted from below the knees and above the head in this magical pass can also be rubbed on the areas of the left and right kidneys.

32. Mixing Energy of the Left and the Right

An inhalation is taken as the hands shake. The left arm reaches diagonally to the extreme right above the head and in line with the right shoulder as an exhalation begins (fig. 78). The hand grabs as if clasping a handful of matter, yanks it out, and brings it to a position above the head and in line with the left shoulder, where the exhalation ends. The left hand remains clasped, and a sharp inhalation is taken as the left arm circles backward (fig. 79), ending in a fisted position at the level of the eyes. The fist is then brought down with an exhalation to the vital center around the pancreas, slowly, but with great force, and the palm rubs softly on that area (fig. 80).

The same movement is repeated with the right arm, but instead of moving in a backward circle, the right arm moves in a frontward circle.

In the belief of shamans, the energy of the two sides of the body is different. The energy of the left is portrayed as being undular, and the energy of the right as being circular. This magical pass is used to apply circular energy to the left and undular energy to the right in order to strengthen the centers of vitality around the liver and pancreas by the inflow of slightly different energy.

Figure 78

Figure 79

Figure 80

33. Grabbing Energy from Above the Head for the Two Vital Centers

Starting at the level of the ear, the left arm circles forward twice (fig. 81) and is then extended over the head, as if to grab something (fig. 82). As this movement is executed, a deep breath is taken, which ends at the moment that the hand grabs upward as if to fetch something above the head. Don Juan recommended that the eyes select, with a quick glance upward, the target for the hand to grab. Whatever is selected and grabbed is then yanked forcefully downward and placed over the vital center around the pancreas and spleen. The air is exhaled at this point. The same movement is

Figure 81

Figure 82

performed with the right arm, and the energy is placed over the center around the liver and gallbladder.

According to shamans, the energy of *intent* tends to gravitate downward, and a more rarefied aspect of the same energy remains in the area above the head. This energy is gathered with this magical pass.

34. Reaching for Energy Above the Head

The left arm is extended upward as far as possible, with the hand open as if to grab something. At the same time, the body is propelled upward with the right leg. When the jump reaches its maximum height, the hand turns inward at the wrist, making a hook with the forearm (fig. 83), which then slowly and forcefully scoops downward. The left hand rubs immediately around the vital center of the pancreas and spleen.

This movement is performed with the right arm in exactly the same fashion as it was done with the left. The right hand immediately brushes across the vital center around the liver and gallbladder.

Figure 83

Shamans believe that the energy stored around the periphery of the luminous sphere that human beings are can be stirred and gathered by jumping forcefully upward. This magical pass is used as a help to dispel problems brought about by concentrating on a given task for long periods of time.

The Fourth Group:
Breathing In the Energy of *Intent*

The three magical passes of this group are for stirring, gathering, and transporting energy for *intent* from three centers—around the feet, on the ankles, and right below the kneecaps—and placing it on the centers of vitality around the kidneys, the liver, the pancreas, the womb, and the genitals. The recommendation to practitioners on the execution of these magical passes is that since they are accompanied by breaths, the inhalations and exhalations should be slow and profound; and that there should be a crystal clear *intent* on the part of the practitioners that the adrenals receive an instantaneous boost while the deep breaths are taken.

35. Dragging Energy from the Kneecaps Along the Front of the Thighs

A deep inhalation is taken as the arms hang by the sides and the hands waver in a continuous tremor, as if stirring a gaseous matter. An exhalation begins as the hands are lifted to the waist, and the palms of the hands strike down in unison, on each side of the body, with great force (fig. 84). The arms are only slightly bent, so that the palms of the hands are a few inches below the stomach. The hands are three or four inches apart, held at ninety-degree angles with the forearms, the fingers pointing forward. Slowly and without touching, the hands make one circle inward toward the front of the body; the muscles of the arms, stomach, and legs are fully contracted (fig. 85). A second circle is drawn in the same fashion as the air is totally expelled through clenched teeth.

Another deep inhalation is taken, and the air is slowly exhaled as three more inward circles are drawn in front of the body. The hands are then retrieved to the front of the hips, and they slide down the front of the thighs with the heels of the palms, fingers slightly turned up, all the

Figure 84   *Figure 85*   *Figure 86*

way to the kneecaps. The air is fully exhaled then. A third deep inhalation is taken while the tips of the fingers press the bottom of the kneecaps. The head is held facing downward, in line with the spine (fig. 86). Then, as the bent knees are straightened, the hands, with the fingers clawed, are dragged up the thighs to the hips, as the air is slowly exhaled. With the last portion of the exhalation, the hands are then brushed on the respective centers of vitality around the pancreas and the liver.

36. Dragging Energy from the Sides of the Legs

A deep inhalation is taken as the hands, held by the sides of the body, shake with a continuous tremor. The hands strike down exactly as in the previous magical pass. An exhalation begins there, while the hands draw, in a similar fashion, two small outward circles by the sides of the body. The muscles of the arms, stomach, and legs are tensed to the maximum. The elbows are held tight but slightly bent (fig. 87).

After the two circles have been drawn, all the air is expelled, and a deep inhalation is taken. Three more outward circles are drawn as the air is slowly exhaled. The hands are then brought to the sides of the hips. The fingers are slightly raised as the heels of the hands rub all the way down the sides of the legs until the fingers reach the outside knobs of the ankles. The head is facing downward, in line with the body (fig. 88). The exhalation ends there, and a deep inhalation is taken with the index and

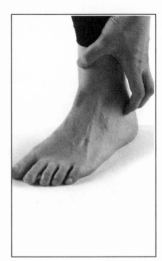

Figure 87   Figure 88   Figure 89

middle fingers pressing the bottom of the knobs (fig. 89). A slow exhalation begins as the hands, with the fingers clawed, are dragged up the sides of the legs to the hips. The exhalation is completed while the palms are brushed on the two respective centers of vitality.

37. Dragging Energy from the Front of the Legs

Again, a deep inhalation is taken as the hands, held by the sides of the body, are shaken. Both arms make a circle by the sides of the body, beginning toward the back, and going over the head (fig. 90) to strike forcefully in front of the body with the palms down and the fingers pointing forward. A slow exhalation begins there, while the hands, starting with the left, move forward and backward three times in alternating succession, as if sliding over a smooth surface. The exhalation ends when the heels of both hands are touching the rib cage (fig. 91). A deep inhalation is taken then. The left hand moves in a sliding motion to the left followed by the right hand sliding to the right; this sequence is executed a total of three times in alternating succession. They end with the heels of the palms against the rib cage, the thumbs

Figure 90　　　　　　　　*Figure 91*　　　　　　　　*Figure 92*

nearly touching each other (fig. 92). Next, both hands are made to slide down the front of the legs until they reach the tendons on the front of the ankles (fig. 93). The exhalation ends there. A deep inhalation is taken as the tendon is tensed by lifting the big toe until the tendon seems to pop up; the index and middle fingers of each hand vibrate the tendons by pressing on them (fig. 94). With the fingers clawed, the hands are dragged up the front of the legs to the hips as a slow exhalation begins. The palms are gently rubbed on the centers of vitality as the exhalation ends.

Figure 93

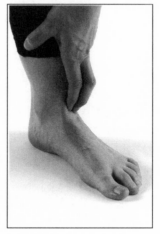

Figure 94

The Series for the Womb

According to don Juan Matus, one of the most specific interests of the shamans who lived in Mexico in ancient times was what they called *the liberation of the womb*. He explained that the liberation of the womb entailed the awakening of its secondary functions, and that since the primary function of the womb, under normal circumstances, was reproduction, those sorcerers were solely concerned with what they considered to be its secondary function: evolution. Evolution, in the case of the womb, was, for them, the awakening and full exploitation of the womb's capacity to process direct knowledge—that is to say, the possibility of apprehending sensory data and interpreting it directly, without the aid of the processes of interpretation with which we are familiar.

For shamans, the moment in which practitioners are transformed from beings that are socialized to reproduce into beings capable of evolving is the moment when they become conscious of *seeing* energy as it flows in the universe. In the opinion of shamans, females can *see* energy directly more readily than males because of the effect of their wombs. It is also their opinion that under normal conditions, regardless of the facility that women have, it is nearly impossible for women or for men to become deliberately conscious that they can *see* energy directly. The reason for this incapacity is something which shamans consider to be a travesty: the fact that there is no one to point out to human beings that it is natural for them to *see* energy directly.

Shamans maintain that women, because they have a womb, are so versatile, so individualistic in their ability to *see* energy directly that this accomplishment, which should be a triumph of the human spirit, is taken for granted. Women are never conscious of their ability. In this respect, males are more proficient. Since it is more difficult for them to *see* energy directly, when they do accomplish this feat, they don't take it for granted. Therefore male sorcerers were the ones who set up the parameters of perceiving energy directly and the ones who tried to describe the phenomenon.

"The basic premise of sorcery," don Juan said to me one day, "discovered by the shamans of my lineage who lived in Mexico in ancient times is that *we are perceivers*. The totality of the human body is an instrument of perception. However, the predominance of the visual in us gives to perception the overall mood of the eyes. This mood, according to the old sorcerers, is merely the heritage of a purely predatorial state.

"The effort of the old sorcerers, which has lasted to our days," don Juan continued, "was geared toward placing themselves beyond the realm of the predator's eye. They conceived the predator's eye to be visual par excellence, and that the realm beyond the predator's eye is the realm of pure perception, which is not visually oriented."

On another occasion, he said that it was a bone of contention for the sorcerers of ancient Mexico that women, who have the organic frame, the womb, that could facilitate their entrance into the realm of pure perception, have no interest in using it. Those shamans viewed it as a woman's paradox to have endless power at her disposal and no interest whatsoever in gaining access to it. However, don Juan had no doubt that this lack of desire to do anything wasn't natural; it was learned.

The aim of the magical passes for the womb is to give the female practitioners of Tensegrity an inkling, which has to be more than an intellectual titillation, of the possibility of canceling out the effect of this noxious socialization that renders women indifferent. Nevertheless, a warning is in order; don Juan Matus advised his female disciples to proceed with great caution when practicing these magical passes. The magical passes for the womb are passes that foster the awakening of the secondary functions of the uterus and ovaries, and those secondary functions are the apprehension of sensory data and the interpretation of them.

Don Juan called the womb *the perceiving box*. He was as convinced as the other sorcerers of his lineage that the uterus and ovaries, if they are pulled out of the reproductive cycle, can become tools of perception, and become indeed the epicenter of evolution. He considered that the first step of evolution is the acceptance of the premise that human beings are perceivers. It was not redundancy on his part to insist ceaselessly that this has to be done before anything else.

"We already know that we are perceivers. What else can we be?" I would say in protest every time he insisted.

"Think about it!" he would reply every time I protested. "Perception plays only a minute role in our lives, and yet, the only thing we are for a fact is perceivers. Human beings apprehend energy at large and turn it into sensory data. Then they interpret these sensory data into the world of everyday life. This interpretation is what we call *perception*.

"The shamans of ancient Mexico, as you already know," don Juan went on, "were convinced that interpretation took place on a point of intense brilliance, the *assemblage point*, which they found when they *saw* the human body as a conglomerate of energy fields that resembled a sphere of luminosity. The advantage of women is their capacity to transfer the interpretation function of the *assemblage point* to the womb. The result of this transfer function is something that cannot be talked about, not because it is something forbidden, but because it is something indescribable.

"The womb," don Juan continued, "is veritably in a chaotic state of turmoil, because of this veiled capacity that exists in remission from the moment of birth until death but which is never utilized. This function of interpretation never ceases to act and yet it has never been raised to the level of full consciousness."

Don Juan's assurance was that the shamans of ancient Mexico, by means of their magical passes, had raised among their female practitioners the interpretive capacity of the womb to the level of consciousness, and by doing this, they had instituted an evolutionary change among them; that is to say, they had turned the womb from an organ of reproduction into the tool of evolution.

Evolution is defined in the world of modern man as the capacity of different species to modify themselves through the processes of natural selection or the transmission of traits, until they can successfully reproduce in their offspring the changes brought about in themselves.

The evolutionary theory that has lasted to our day, from the time it was formulated over a hundred years ago, says that the origin and the perpetuation of a new species of animal or plant is brought about by the process of natural selection, which favors the survival of individuals whose characteristics render them best adapted to their environment, and that evolution is brought about by the interplay of three principles: first, heredity, the conservative force that transmits similar organic forms from one generation to another; second, variation, the differences present in all forms of life; and third, the struggle for existence, which determines which variations confer advantages in a given environment. This last principle gave rise to the phrase still in current use: "the survival of the fittest."

Evolution, as a theory, has enormous loopholes; it leaves tremendous room for doubt. It is at best an open-ended process for which scientists have created classificatory schemes; they have created taxonomies to their hearts' content. But the fact remains that it is a theory full of holes. What we know about evolution doesn't tell us what evolution is.

Don Juan Matus believed that evolution was the product of *intending* at a very profound level. In the case of sorcerers, that profound level was marked by what he had called *inner silence*.

"For instance," he said, when he was explaining this phenomenon, "sorcerers are sure that dinosaurs flew because they *intended* flying. But what is very difficult to understand, much less accept, is that wings are only one solution to flying, in this case, the dinosaurs' solution. Nevertheless, this solution is not the only one that is possible. It's the only one available to us by imitation. Our airplanes are flying with wings imitating the dinosaurs, perhaps because flying has never been *intended* again since the dinosaurs' time. Perhaps wings were adopted because they were the easiest solution."

Don Juan was of the opinion that if we were to *intend* it now, there is no way of knowing what other options for flying would be available besides wings. He insisted that because *intent* is infinite, there was no logical way in which the mind, following processes of deduction or induction, could calculate or determine what these options for flying might be.

The magical passes of the Series for the Womb are extremely potent, and should be practiced sparingly. In ancient times, men were barred from executing them. In more recent times, there has been a tendency among sorcerers to render these magical passes more generic, and thus the possibility arose that they could also be of service to men. This possibility, however, is very delicate and requires careful handling, great concentration, and determination.

The male practitioners of Tensegrity who teach the magical passes have opted, because of their potent effect, to practice them by brushing the energy that they generate only lightly on the area of the genitals themselves. This measure has proven to be enough to provide a beneficial jolt without any profound or deleterious effects.

Don Juan explained that the sorcerers of his lineage, at a given moment, allowed males to practice these magical passes because of the possibility that the energy engendered by them would awaken the secondary function of the male sexual organs. He said that those sorcerers considered that the secondary function of the male sexual organs is not at all similar to that of the womb; no interpretation of sensory data can take place because the male sexual organs hang outside of the cavity of the body. Because of these particular circumstances, their conclusion was that the secondary function of the male organs is something which they termed *evolutionary support:* a sort of springboard that catapults men to perform extraordinary feats of what sorcerers of ancient Mexico called *unbending intent,* or clearheaded purpose and concentration.

The Series for the Womb is divided into four sections which correspond to the three female disciples of don Juan Matus: Taisha Abelar, Florinda Donner-Grau, and Carol Tiggs; and to the Blue Scout, who was born into don Juan's world. The first is composed of three magical passes belonging to Taisha Abelar; the second is composed of one magical pass directly related to Florinda Donner-Grau; the third, of three magical passes that have to do exclusively with Carol Tiggs; and the fourth, of five magical passes that belong to the Blue Scout. The magical passes of each section are pertinent to a specific type of individual. Tensegrity has rendered them capable of being utilized by anybody, although they are still slanted in the direction of the type of person that each of those four women is.

The First Group:
Magical Passes Belonging to Taisha Abelar

The three magical passes of this group are geared to gathering energy for the womb from six specific areas: the left and right front of the body, the left and right sides of the body at the height of the hips, and from behind the shoulder blades and above the head. The explanation that the shamans of ancient Mexico gave was that energy especially suited for the womb accumulates on those areas, and that the movements of these magical passes are the appropriate antennas that gather that energy exclusively.

1. Extracting Energy from the Front of the Body with the Index and Middle Fingers

The first sensation that a Tensegrity practitioner seeks while executing this magical pass is a pressure on the tendons of the back of the hand, a sensation which is obtained by opening the index and middle fingers as far as possible while they are fully extended. The last two fingers are curled over the palm of the hand, and the thumb holds them in place (fig. 95).

The magical pass starts by placing the left foot in front of the body in a T position, perpendicular to the right one. The left arm and the left leg make a series of synchronized forward circling movements. The leg circles by first lifting the ball of the foot, and then the whole foot, and a step is taken that rolls forward in the air and ends on the heel, with the toes up, as the body leans forward, creating pressure on a muscle on the front of the left calf.

In synchronization with this movement, the left arm rotates forward over the head, also making a complete circle. The index and middle fingers are fully extended, and the palm faces to the right. The pressure on the tendons of the back of the hand has to be maintained with maximum stress during the entire movement (fig. 96). At the end of the third circling movement of the arm and foot, the entire foot is placed on the ground with a forceful stomp, shifting the weight of the body forward. At the same time, the arm shoots out in a stabbing motion, with the index and middle fingers fully extended and the palm of the hand

Figure 95

Figure 96

Figure 97

facing right; the muscles of the entire left side of the body are kept tense and contracted (fig. 97).

An undulating movement is made, as if drawing, with the two extended fingers pointing forward, a letter S that is lying on its side. The wrist is bent so that the fingers point upward once the S is completed (fig. 98). Next, the wrist bends so the fingers again point forward and the S is cut in half with a horizontal stroke of the two fingers from right to left. Then the wrist is bent so the two fingers point upward once more, and a sweeping movement is made from left to right with the palm turned toward the face. The palm of the hand is turned to face outward, as the arm sweeps from right to left. The left arm is retrieved to the level of the chest, and two forward stabbing motions are executed with the fingers fully extended and the palm of the hand facing downward. The palm of the hand is turned toward the face once more, and the hand sweeps again from left to right and from right to left, exactly as before.

The body leans back slightly, shifting the weight to the back leg. Then the hand, with the two fingers curved like a claw, reaches out at waist level in front of the body as if to grab something, contracting the muscles and tendons of the forearm and hand as if forcefully extracting some heavy substance (fig. 99). The clawed hand is retrieved to the side of the body. All the fingers of the hand are then fully extended, with the thumb locked and the fingers separated at the middle and fourth

Figure 98   *Figure 99*   *Figure 100*

fingers, making a letter V, which is brushed over the womb, or over the sexual organs, in the case of men (fig. 100).

A quick jump is made to shift legs, so that the right foot is in front of the left one, again making a T. The same movements are repeated with the right arm and leg.

2. Jumping to Stir Energy for the Womb and Grabbing It with the Hand
This magical pass begins by placing the right foot perpendicular to the left one in a T position. A tap is made with the right heel; this tap serves as an impulse for a small hop of the right foot which ends with the right toes pointing forward, followed immediately by a one-step lateral hop of the left foot that ends with the left heel on the ground, perpendicular to the right foot. The rest of the left foot touches the ground, shifting the weight to the left leg, as the left arm moves in a grabbing motion to clasp something in front of the body with a clawed hand (fig. 101). The hand then rubs gently on the area of the left ovary.

A tap of the left heel serves as an impulse for a sequence of movements that is a mirror image of the preceding ones.

Energy stirred up by the motion of the feet in this magical pass bounces upward, is caught with each hand in turn, and is placed over the uterus and the left and the right ovaries.

Figure 101

3. Slapping Energy on the Ovaries
The third magical pass begins by circling the left arm over the head, to the back, in toward the shoulder blades, and out again to the front until it reaches the level of the chin; the palm faces up. The hand draws another circle that goes up and over toward the right; it continues downward, all the way to the right waist and then sweeps upward over the head, completing the figure of a number eight. The palm flips to face the front (fig. 102). Then the hand descends forcefully, as if slapping the area just in front of the left ovary (fig. 103). The hand then brushes gently on the area of the left ovary.

The same pattern is repeated with the right arm.

Figure 102   Figure 103

The Second Group:
A Magical Pass Directly Related
to Florinda Donner-Grau

In this group, there is only one magical pass. The effect of this magical pass is utterly congruous with the personality of Florinda Donner-Grau. Don Juan Matus regarded her as being very straightforward, so to-the-point that sometimes her directness became unbearable. Her activities in the sorcerers' world, as a consequence of her directness, have always been geared toward the goal of evolution, or the transformation of the womb from a receptacle and promoter of fertility to an organ of awareness, through which thoughts which are not part of our normal cognition can be processed.

4. Sphinx Paws
This magical pass begins with a quick, deep inhalation. The air is sharply exhaled with a forceful strike of the wrists to the front of the body. This is achieved with the hands turned downward sharply, at right angles to the forearms; the fingers point to the ground, and the striking surface is the backs of the hands at the wrists.

The hands are pulled upward to the level of the shoulders, the palms facing forward, in a straight line with the forearms. A deep inhalation is taken. The hands are held in this position as the trunk turns to the left. The hands then strike, with the palms down, to the level of the hips (fig. 104). The air is exhaled sharply. The hands are raised above the shoulders again as the trunk turns to the front, and a deep inhalation is taken. With the hands still above the shoulders, the trunk is turned to the right. Next both hands strike, with the palms down, to the level of the hips as the air is exhaled.

Both hands move then to the right of the body, with the palms slightly cupped and turned to the left, as if to scoop a liquid substance. Both arms move from right to left to right, drawing the figure of a reclining number eight in front of the body. This is achieved by first moving the arms all the way to the left, following a twist of the waist, and then returning back to the right, following a reverse twist of the waist. The slightly cupped palms are turned to face the right, as if to continue scooping a liquid substance in the opposite direction (fig. 105).

As the figure eight is completed, the left hand stops to rest on the left hip, while the right arm continues moving to the right; the arm goes up over the head and makes a big loop to the back that ends when the hand is brought back to the front, to the level of the chin; the palm of the hand faces up. The hand continues moving, making another loop to the left, going in front of the face, over the left shoulder. Next it moves in a straight line across the body at the level of the hip, cutting through the figure eight (fig. 106). From there, the palm moves back toward the

Figure 104   Figure 105   Figure 106

body and is made to slide over the right ovary, as if the hand were a knife that comes to rest in its sheath.

The exact same movements are performed, but striking to the right side of the body first, in order to allow the left arm to execute the last movement.

The Third Group:
Magical Passes That Have to Do
Exclusively with Carol Tiggs

The three magical passes of the third group deal with the energy that is directly on the area of the womb. This emphasis makes these three magical passes extraordinarily potent. Moderation is strongly recommended in order to bring the sensations of awakening the womb to a manageable level. In this fashion the linear-minded interpretation of these sensations as premenstrual pangs or heaviness on the ovaries can be avoided.

Don Juan Matus told his three female disciples that the secondary functions of the womb, upon being awakened by the appropriate magical passes, give the sensorial input of discomfort, but that what takes place at an energetic level is the influx of energy into the vortex of the womb. Energy which has, up to this point, remained unused and on the periphery of the luminous sphere is suddenly dropped into that vortex.

5. Packing Energy on the Womb

The first magical pass begins by bringing the two hands to the area of the womb. The wrists are bent sharply, and the hands are cupped, the fingers pointing to the womb.

The two hands are extended so that the tips of the fingers point toward each other. Then they make an ample circle, first going upward and out, and then down, with both hands together, ending right over the womb (fig. 107). Next, the hands separate to the width of the body (fig. 108), and are brought forcefully toward the center of the womb as if a thick ball were being squashed. The same movement is repeated, and the hands are brought closer together, as if the ball were being further squashed. Then it is torn apart by a powerful movement of the hands, which grab and rip (fig. 109). The hands are then brushed over the area of the uterus and the ovaries.

Figure 107　　　　　*Figure 108*　　　　　*Figure 109*

6. Stirring and Guiding Energy Directly into the Womb

This magical pass begins with an exhalation as the arms are stretched out in front of the body, with the backs of the hands touching. A deep breath is taken as the arms move laterally away from each other, drawing half-circles which end with the forearms touching in front of the body at the level of the chest, and the arms extended forward with the elbows slightly bent. The palms face up. Then the trunk bends forward slightly as the forearms move backward so that the elbows are moored on the solar plexus with the forearms still touching, side by side (fig. 110). Next, a slow exhalation begins, which must last through the following movements: The back side of the left wrist is placed on top of the inner side of the right wrist, maneuvering the arms to make the figure of the letter X; the wrists rotate so that the palms circle in toward the body, and then back out to face front, without losing the X shape of the wrists; the left hand ends up on top of the right one (fig. 111). The hands are made into fists and separated vigorously (fig. 112), and then brought to the area of the left and right ovaries as the exhalation ends.

Figure 110

Figure 111

Figure 112

7. Squeezing Out Injurious Energy from the Ovaries

The left hand is held in front of the body with the palm up. The elbow is bent at a right angle and tucked against the rib cage. The index and middle fingers of the left hand are extended while the thumb holds the other two fingers against the palm. The two extended fingers of the left hand are grabbed from underneath by the right hand, and squeezed as if drawing something from the base of the two extended fingers of the left hand and making it move to the tips (fig. 113). Then the right hand shakes

Figure 113

Figure 114

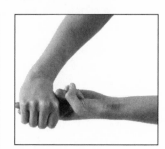

Figure 115

vigorously whatever it drew from those two fingers with a backhanded, downward striking motion on the right side of the body. The left thumb releases the other two fingers, and the hand is held in a letter V shape, with the index and middle fingers together, and the fourth and fifth fingers together. The palm of the hand is lightly brushed over the area of the left ovary. The same movements are repeated with the right hand.

For the second part of this magical pass, the trunk is bent sharply forward. The left arm hangs in between the legs, the elbow cushioned against the umbilical region. Exactly the same movements performed in the first part of the magical pass are executed again, except this time the two extended fingers of the left hand are grabbed by the right hand from above (figs. 114, 115). The same movements are repeated on the right.

The Fourth Group:
Magical Passes That Belong to the Blue Scout

The magical passes of this group are the natural conclusion of the whole series. An impersonal mood is the driving force of this group of passes. The inhalations and exhalations are sharp, but not deep, and the movements are accompanied by an explosive hissing sound of air being expelled.

The value of the Blue Scout's magical passes resides in the capacity of each of them to give the womb the hardness that it requires in order to arrive at its secondary functions, which can be easily defined, in the case of the Blue Scout, as the ability to be alert without pause. The criticism of sorcerers about our normal state of being is that we seem to be perennially on automatic pilot; we say things that we don't mean to say, we ignore things that we shouldn't ignore. In other words, we are aware of what surrounds us only in very short spurts. Most of the time, we function on sheer momentum, habit, and that habit is, in essence, to be oblivious to everything. The idea of the sorcerers of ancient Mexico was that, in women, the womb is the organ that can resolve this impasse, and for that, it needs to acquire hardness.

8. Drawing Energy from the Front with Insect Antennas
The index and middle fingers are held by the sides of the chest in a letter V position, while the thumbs press the other two fingers against the palms; the palms are up (fig. 116). Next, the palms turn downward, and

the two fingers strike out in front of the body, as a sharp exhalation is made, with clenched teeth and a hissing, whistlelike sound (fig. 117). A deep inhalation is taken as the hands are retrieved with the palms up to the sides of the chest. The same movement is repeated one more time, and the palms of the hands are brushed on the area of the ovaries, with the fingers separated between the middle and fourth fingers.

Figure 116   Figure 117

9. Drawing Energy from the Sides at an Angle

This magical pass begins by pivoting on the right foot and putting the left leg in front, at a forty-five-degree angle. The right foot is the horizontal bar of the letter T, and the left foot, the vertical. The body rocks back and forth. Then the left elbow is bent, and the hand is brought to the level of the chest with the palm up. The index and middle fingers are held in the shape of the letter V. The thumb holds the other two fingers against the palm (fig. 118). A strike is made, leaning the body forward sharply. The palm of the hand turns down as the fingers strike. The air is exhaled with a hiss (fig. 119). An inhalation is taken as the hand retrieves to the side of the chest with the palm up. The palm of the hand is then lightly brushed on the left ovary, with the fingers separated between the middle and fourth fingers.

A jump is taken to switch feet and face a new direction to the right, still at a forty-five-degree angle. The same movements are repeated with the right arm.

Figure 118   Figure 119

10. Drawing Energy Laterally with an Insect Cut

The hands are held on the sides of the chest, with the index and middle fingers of each hand in a V shape and the thumbs holding the other two fingers against the palms. The palms face up. Remaining at the level of the chest, the hands are pivoted on the heels of the palms and brought to face each other. Next, a hissing exhalation is made as both arms are fully extended laterally, with the palms facing the front. The index and middle fingers are moved with a cutting motion as if they were indeed

Figure 120   Figure 121

scissors, as the exhalation ends in a whistlelike fashion (fig. 120).

An inhalation is taken as the arms are retrieved; the elbows are down, and the arms come to rest on the sides of the body by the chest, hands pointing sideways (fig. 121). Next the hands are pivoted on the heel of the palm so the index and middle fingers point to the front. The fingers are then separated at the middle and fourth fingers, and a hissing exhalation is made as the palms of the hands brush over the area of the ovaries.

11. Drilling Energy from Between the Feet with Each Hand

A deep inhalation is taken. A long hissing exhalation follows while the left hand descends with a rotating movement of the wrist, which makes the hand resemble a drill that seems to perforate a substance in front of the body between the legs. Then the index and middle fingers make a two-pronged claw and grab something from the area between the feet (fig. 122) and pull it upward, with a deep inhalation, to the level of the hips. The arm moves over the head to the back of the body and the palm is placed on the area of the left kidney and adrenal (fig. 123).

The left hand is held there while the right hand performs the same movements. Once the right hand is placed on the area of the right kidney and adrenal, an inhalation is taken. The left hand moves over the head to the front of the body, and brushes, with the fingers separated at the middle and fourth fingers, over the left ovary. This movement of the

Figure 122

Figure 123

arm from back to front is accompanied by the whistlelike sound of a sharp exhalation. Another deep inhalation is taken, and the right hand is brought to the right ovary in the same fashion.

12. Drilling Energy from Between the Feet with Both Hands

This magical pass is similar to the preceding one, except that instead of performing the movements separately, the hands execute the drilling movements in unison. Then the index and middle fingers of both hands make two-pronged claws, and grab something from the area between the feet at the same time. They return to the level of the hips, and then circle around the sides of the body to the area of the kidneys and adrenals; a deep breath is taken as the palms rub those areas (fig. 124). Then an exhalation is made as the arms draw another circle around the sides of the body to the front to brush the area over the left and right ovaries with the fingers of each hand separated at the middle. Again, this movement of the arms from back to front is accompanied by a whistlelike exhalation.

Figure 124

The Series of the Five Concerns: The Westwood Series

One of the most important series for the practitioners of Tensegrity is called *The Series of the Five Concerns*. A nickname for this series is *The Westwood Series*, given to it because it was taught publicly for the first time in the Pauley Pavilion at the University of California at Los Angeles, which is located in an area called Westwood. This series was conceived as an attempt to integrate what don Juan Matus called *the five concerns of the shamans of ancient Mexico*. Everything those sorcerers did rotated around five concerns: one, the magical passes; two, the energetic center in the human body called the *center for decisions*; three, *recapitulation*, the means for enhancing the scope of human awareness; four, *dreaming*, the bona fide art of breaking the parameters of normal perception; five, *inner silence*, the stage of human perception from which those sorcerers launched every one of their perceptual attainments. This sequence of five concerns was an arrangement patterned on the understanding that those sorcerers had of the world around them.

One of the astounding findings of those shamans, according to what don Juan taught, was the existence in the universe of an agglutinating force that binds energy fields together into concrete, functional units. The sorcerers who discovered the existence of this force described it as a vibration, or a vibratory condition, that permeates groups of energy fields and glues them together.

In terms of this arrangement of the five concerns of the shamans of ancient Mexico, the magical passes fulfill the function of the vibratory condition those shamans talked about. When those sorcerers put together this shamanistic sequence of five concerns, they copied the patterning of energy that was revealed to them when they were capable of *seeing* energy as it flows in the universe. The binding force was the magical passes. The magical passes were the unit that permeated through the four remaining units and grouped them together into one functional whole.

The Westwood Series, following the patterning of the shamans of ancient Mexico, has consequently been divided into four groups, arranged in terms of their importance as envisioned by the sorcerers who formulated them: one, the *center for decisions*; two, *recapitulation*; three, *dreaming*; four, *inner silence*.

The First Group:
The *Center for Decisions*

The most important topic for the shamans who lived in Mexico in ancient times, and for all the shamans of don Juan's lineage, was the *center for decisions*. Shamans are convinced, by the practical results of their endeavors, that there is a spot on the human body which accounts for decision making, *the V spot*—the area on the crest of the sternum at the base of the neck, where the clavicles meet to form a letter V. It is a center where energy is rarefied to the point of being tremendously subtle, and it stores a specific type of energy which shamans are incapable of defining. They are utterly certain, however, that they can feel the presence of that energy, and its effects. It is the belief of shamans that this special energy is always pushed out of that center very early in the lives of human beings, and it never returns to it, thus depriving human beings of something perhaps more important than all the energy of the other centers combined: the capacity to make decisions.

In relation to the issue of making decisions, don Juan expressed the hard opinion of the sorcerers of his lineage. Their observations, over the centuries, had led them to conclude that human beings are incapable of making decisions, and that for this reason, they have created the social order: gigantic institutions that assume responsibility for decision making. They let those gigantic institutions decide for them, and they merely fulfill the decisions already made on their behalf.

The V spot at the base of the neck was, for those shamans, a place of such importance that they rarely touched it with their hands; if it was touched, the touch was ritualistic and always performed by someone else with the aid of an object. They used highly polished pieces of hardwood or polished bones of animals, utilizing the round head of the bone so as to have an object of the perfect contour, the size of the hollow spot on the neck. They would press with those bones or pieces of wood to create pressure on the borders of that hollow spot. Those objects were also used, although rarely, for self-massage, or for what we understand nowadays as acupressure.

"How did they come to find out that that hollow spot is the *center for decisions?*" I asked don Juan once.

"Every center of energy in the body," he replied, "shows a concentration of energy; a sort of vortex of energy, like a funnel that actually seems to rotate counterclockwise from the perspective of the seer who gazes into it. The strength of a particular center depends on the force of that movement. If it barely moves, the center is exhausted, depleted of energy.

"When the sorcerers of ancient times," don Juan continued, "were scanning the body with their *seeing* eye, they noticed the presence of those vortexes. They became very curious about them, and made a map of them."

"Are there many such centers in the body, don Juan?" I asked.

"There are hundreds of them," he replied, "if not thousands! One can say that a human being is nothing else but a conglomerate of thousands of twirling vortexes, some of them so very small that they are, let's say, like pinholes, but very important pinholes. Most of the vortexes are vortexes of energy. Energy flows freely through them, or is stuck in them. There are, however, six which are so enormous that they deserve special treatment. They are centers of life and vitality. Energy there is never stuck, but sometimes the supply of energy is so scarce that the center barely rotates."

Don Juan explained that those enormous centers of vitality were located on six areas of the body. He enumerated them in terms of the importance that shamans accorded them. The first was on the area of the liver and gallbladder; the second on the area of the pancreas and spleen; the third on the area of the kidneys and adrenals; and the fourth on the hollow spot at the base of the neck on the frontal part of the body. The fifth was around the womb, and the sixth was on the top of the head.

The fifth center, pertinent only to women, had, according to what don Juan said, a special kind of energy that gave sorcerers the impression of liquidness. It was a feature that only some women had. It seemed to serve as a natural filter that screened out superfluous influences.

The sixth center, located on top of the head, don Juan described as something more than an anomaly, and refrained absolutely from having anything to do with it. He portrayed it as possessing not a circular vortex of energy, like the others, but a pendulumlike, back-and-forth movement somehow reminiscent of the beating of a heart.

"Why is the energy of that center so different, don Juan?" I asked him.

"That sixth center of energy," he said, "doesn't quite belong to man. You see, we human beings are under siege, so to speak. That center has been taken over by an invader, an unseen predator. And the only way to overcome this predator is by fortifying all the other centers."

"Isn't it a bit paranoiac to feel that we are under siege, don Juan?" I asked.

"Well, maybe for you, but certainly not for me," he replied. "I *see* energy, and I *see* that the energy over the center on the top of the head doesn't fluctuate like the energy of the other centers. It has a back-and-forth movement, quite disgusting, and quite foreign. I also *see* that in a sorcerer who has been capable of vanquishing the mind, which sorcerers call a *foreign installation*, the fluctuation of that center has become exactly like the fluctuation of all the others."

Don Juan, throughout the years of my apprenticeship, systematically refused to talk about that sixth center. On this occasion when he was telling me about the centers of vitality, he dismissed my frantic probes, rather rudely, and began to talk about the fourth center, the *center for decisions*.

"This fourth center," he said, "has a special type of energy, which appears to the eye of the seer as possessing a unique transparency, something that could be described as resembling water: energy so fluid that it seems liquid. The liquid appearance of this special energy is the mark of a filterlike quality of the *center for decisions* itself, which screens any energy coming to it, and draws from it only the aspect of it that is liquidlike. Such a quality of liquidness is a uniform and consistent feature of this center. Sorcerers also call it *the watery center*.

"The rotation of the energy at the *center for decisions* is the weakest of them all," he went on. "That's why man can rarely decide anything. Sorcerers *see* that after they practice certain magical passes, that center becomes active, and they can certainly make decisions to their hearts' content, while they couldn't even take a first step before."

Don Juan was quite emphatic about the fact that the shamans of ancient Mexico had an aversion that bordered on phobia about touching their own hollow spot at the base of the neck. The only way in which they accepted any interference whatsoever with that spot was through the use of their magical passes, which reinforce that center by bringing dispersed energy to it, clearing away, in this manner, any hesitation in decision making born out of the natural energy dispersion brought about by the wear and tear of everyday life.

"A human being," don Juan said, "perceived as a conglomerate of energy fields, is a concrete and sealed unit into which no energy can be injected, and from which no energy can escape. The feeling of losing energy, which all of us experience at one time or another, is the result of energy being chased away, dispersed from the five enormous natural centers of life and vitality. Any sense of gaining energy is due to the *redeployment of energy* previously dispersed from those centers. That is to say, the energy is relocated onto those five centers of life and vitality."

THE MAGICAL PASSES FOR THE CENTER FOR DECISIONS

1. Bringing Energy to the *Center for Decisions* with a Back-and-Forth Motion of the Hands and Arms with the Palms Turned Downward

The arms shoot out to the front at a forty-five-degree angle with an exhalation, the palms of the hands facing down (fig. 125). Then they are retrieved to the sides of the chest, under the axilla, with an inhalation. The shoulders are raised in order to maintain the same degree of

Figure 125

Figure 126

inclination (fig. 126). In the second facet of this movement, the arms are extended downward with an inhalation, and pulled back with an exhalation.

Figure 127

2. Bringing Energy to the *Center for Decisions* with a Back-and-Forth Motion of the Hands and Arms with the Palms Turned Upward

This magical pass is like the preceding one, and it is executed in exactly the same fashion, except that it is done with the palms of the hands turned upward (fig. 127). The inhalations and exhalations are also exactly as in the preceding movement. Air is exhaled as the hands and arms move forward at a forty-five-degree level of inclination, and it is inhaled as the arms move backward. Then air is inhaled as the hands and arms move downward, and exhaled as the hands and arms retrieve.

Figure 128

3. Bringing Energy to the *Center for Decisions* with a Circular Motion of the Hands and Arms with the Palms Turned Downward

This magical pass begins exactly like the first one of this group, except that when the hands reach their fully extended position, two complete circles are drawn with the hands and the arms going away from each other to reach a point about six inches beyond the rib cage. When the hands complete the circles (fig. 128), the arms are retrieved to the sides of the rib cage under the axilla.

This magical pass consists of two facets. In the first, air is exhaled as the circles are drawn and inhaled as the arms are retrieved backward. In the second, air is inhaled as the hands and arms draw the circles and exhaled as the arms are retrieved.

4. Bringing Energy to the *Center for Decisions* in a Circular Motion of the Hands and Arms with the Palms Turned Upward

This magical pass is exactly like the preceding one, with the same two facets of inhalation and exhalation, but the two circles are drawn by the hands and arms with the palms of the hands turned upward (fig. 129).

Figure 129

5. Bringing Energy to the *Center for Decisions* from the Midsection of the Body

The arms are bent at the elbows and kept high, at the level of the shoulders. The fingers are kept loosely pointing toward the V spot, but without touching it (fig. 130). The arms move in a teeter-totter fashion from right to left and left to right. The motion is not accomplished by moving the shoulders or the hips, but by the contraction of the muscles of the stomach, which moves the midsection to the right, to the left, and to the right again, and so on.

6. Bringing Energy to the *Center for Decisions* from the Area of the Shoulder Blades

The arms are bent, as in the previous movement, but the shoulders are rounded so that the elbows are heavily drawn toward the front. The left hand is placed on top of the right. The fingers are held loose, pointing toward the V spot without touching it, and the chin juts out and rests on the hollow spot between the thumb and index finger of the left hand (fig. 131). The bent elbows are pushed forward, extending the shoulder blades, one at a time, to the maximum.

Figure 130

7. Stirring Energy Around the *Center for Decisions* with a Bent Wrist

Both hands are brought to the V spot on the base of the neck, without touching it. The hands are gently curved; the fingers point at the *center for decisions*. Then the hands begin to move, the left first, followed by the right, as if stirring a liquid substance around that area, or as if they were fanning air into

Figure 131

the V spot with a series of gentle movements of each hand; these movements are accomplished by extending the whole arm laterally and then bringing it back to the area in front of the V spot (fig. 132). Then the left arm strikes out in front of the V spot, with the hand turned sharply inward, using the wrist and the back of the hand as a striking surface (fig. 133). The right arm executes the same movement. In this manner, a series of forceful blows are delivered to the area right in front of the V spot.

Figure 132

Figure 133

8. Transferring Energy from the Two Centers of Vitality on the Front of the Body to the *Center for Decisions*

Both hands are brought to the area of the pancreas and spleen, a few inches in front of the body. The left hand, with the palm turned upward, is held four or five inches below the right one, which has the palm turned downward. The left forearm is held at a ninety-degree angle, extended straight out to the front. The right forearm is also at a ninety-degree angle, but held close to the body, so that the fingertips point to the left (fig. 134). The left hand makes two inward circles about a foot in diameter around the area of the pancreas and spleen. Once it has completed the second circle, the right hand shoots out to the front and strikes with the edge of the hand, to the area an arm's length in front of the liver and gallbladder (fig. 135).

The exact same movements are performed on the other side of the body by reversing the position of the hands, which are brought to the

Figure 134

Figure 135

area of the liver and gallbladder, with the right hand circling and the left hand striking forward to the area an arm's length in front of the pancreas and spleen.

9. Bringing Energy to the *Center for Decisions* from the Knees

The left hand and arm draw two circles about a foot in diameter in front of the V spot, a bit toward the left (fig. 136). The palm of the hand is facing downward. Once the second circle has been drawn, the forearm is raised to the level of the shoulder and the hand strikes away from the face, diagonally to the right, at the level of the V spot, with a flick of the wrist, as if holding a whip (fig. 137). The same movements are performed with the right hand.

Then a deep inhalation is taken, and an exhalation follows as the hands and arms slide downward until they reach the tops of the knees, with the palms facing up. A deep inhalation is taken there and the arms are raised, with the left arm in the lead; the right arm crosses over the left as they go over the head until the fingers rest on the back of the neck. The breath is held as the top of the trunk moves three times in succession in a teeter-totter motion; the left shoulder goes down first, then the right, and so on (fig. 138). Then the air is exhaled as the arms and hands move back downward to the

Figure 136

Figure 137   Figure 138   Figure 139

tops of the knees, again with the palms of the hands facing up.

A deep inhalation is taken, and then the air is exhaled as the hands are raised from the knees to the level of the V spot, with the fingers pointing toward it, without touching it (fig. 139). The hands are brought once more to the knees with an exhalation. A final deep inhalation is taken and the hands are raised to the level of the eyes, and then brought down to the sides as the air is exhaled.

The next three magical passes, according to don Juan, transfer energy which belongs only to the *center for decisions* from the frontal edge of the luminous sphere, where it has accumulated over the years, to the back, and then from the back of the luminous sphere to the front. He said that this energy transferred back and forth goes through the V spot, which acts as a filter, utilizing only the energy that is proper to it and discarding the rest. He pointed out that because of this selective process of the V spot, it is essential to perform these three magical passes as many times as possible.

10. Energy Going Through the *Center for Decisions* from the Front to the Back and the Back to the Front with Two Blows
A deep inhalation is taken. Then the air is slowly exhaled as the left arm strikes out at the level of the solar plexus, with the palm of the hand turned upward; the palm is held flat and the fingers are together.

Then the hand is clasped into a fist. The arm moves to the back, striking from the height of the hips with a backhand blow (fig. 140). The exhalation ends as the hand opens.

Another deep inhalation is taken. A slow exhalation follows while the palm of the open hand, still in back of the body, taps ten times as if lightly hitting a solid round object. Then the hand is clasped into a fist before the arm moves to the front in a swinglike punch that strikes an area in front of the V spot, an arm's length away from it (fig. 141). The hand opens as if releasing something held in it. The arm moves down, back, and then over the head and strikes with the palm down in front of the V spot, as if breaking whatever it has released. The exhalation ends then (fig. 142).

The same sequence of movements is repeated with the right arm.

Figure 140   Figure 141   Figure 142

11. Transferring Energy from the Front to the Back and the Back to the Front with the Hook of the Arm

A deep inhalation is made. Then the air is slowly exhaled as the left arm moves forward with the palm of the hand turned upward. The hand is quickly clasped into a fist. The fisted hand rotates until the back of the hand is turned upward and strikes over the shoulder to the back. The fisted palm faces upward. The hand opens and turns to face downward, and the exhalation ends.

Another deep inhalation is taken. Then a slow exhalation begins as the hand, made into a downward hook, scoops three times, as if rolling a solid substance into a ball (fig. 143). The ball is tossed upward to the level of the head with a flick of the hand and forearm (fig. 144), and quickly grabbed with the hand bent again at the wrist like a hook (fig. 145). The arm moves to the front, then to the height of the right shoulder and strikes forward to an area right in front of the V spot an arm's length away from it, using the wrist and the back of the hand as a strik-

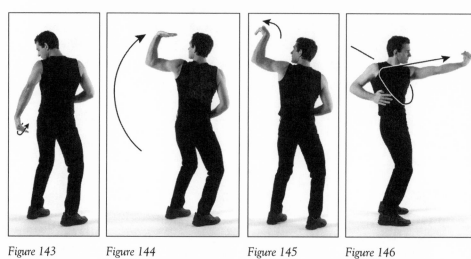

Figure 143   Figure 144   Figure 145   Figure 146

ing surface (fig. 146). The hand then opens as if to release whatever it had trapped, and the arm moves down to the back and over the head to strike it with great force with the flat palm. The exhalation ends as the whole body shakes with the force of the strike.

The same movements are repeated with the other arm.

12. Transferring Energy from the Front to the Back and the Back to the Front with Three Blows

A deep inhalation is taken. A slow exhalation follows as the left arm strikes forward with the hand open, the flat palm turned upward. The hand is quickly clasped into a fist, and the arm retrieves as if to deliver an elbow blow to the back. Then it moves laterally to the right and delivers a side punch with the forearm rubbing on the body (fig. 147). The elbow is retrieved again as if to deliver an elbow blow to the back. The arm is extended and moved out to the left side and to the back, to deliver the fourth blow behind the body with the back of the fisted hand. The exhalation ends as the hand opens (fig. 148).

A deep inhalation is taken again. A slow exhalation follows as the hand, bent downward into a hook, scoops three times. Then the hand grabs as if it were clasping something solid (fig. 149). The arm swings to the front at the level of the *center for decisions*. It continues to the right shoulder; there the forearm makes a loop upward and delivers a back-fist blow to the area in front of the V spot, an arm's length away from it (fig. 150). The hand opens as if to release something that it was clasping. Then it moves down, goes behind the body, comes above the head, with the palm of the hand down, and smashes whatever it released with a forceful blow of the open hand. The slow exhalation ends there (fig. 151).

The same movements are repeated with the right arm.

Figure 147

Figure 148

Figure 149

Figure 150

Figure 151

The Second Group:
The *Recapitulation*

The *recapitulation*, according to what don Juan taught his disciples, was a technique discovered by the sorcerers of ancient Mexico, and used by every shaman practitioner from then on, to view and relive all the experiences of their lives, in order to achieve two transcendental goals: one, the abstract goal of fulfilling a universal code that demands that awareness must be relinquished at the moment of death; and two, the extremely pragmatic goal of acquiring perceptual fluidity.

He said that the formulation of their first goal was the result of observations that those sorcerers made by means of their capacity to *see* energy directly as it flows in the universe. They had *seen* that there exists in the universe a gigantic force, an immense conglomerate of energy fields which they called *the Eagle*, or the *dark sea of awareness*. They observed that the *dark sea of awareness* is the force that lends awareness to all living beings, from viruses to men. They believed that it lends awareness to a newborn being, and that this being enhances that awareness by means of its life experiences until a moment in which the force demands its return.

In the understanding of those sorcerers, all living beings die because they are forced to return the awareness lent to them. Sorcerers throughout the ages have understood that there is no way for what modern man calls our linear mode of thinking to explain such a phenomenon, because there is no room for a cause-and-effect line of reasoning as to why and how awareness is lent and then taken back. The sorcerers of ancient Mexico viewed it as an *energetic fact* of the universe, a fact that can't be explained in terms of cause and effect, or in terms of a purpose which can be determined a priori.

The sorcerers of don Juan's lineage believed that to *recapitulate* meant to give the *dark sea of awareness* what it was seeking: their life experiences. They believed that by means of the *recapitulation*, however, they could acquire a degree of control that could permit them to separate their life experiences from their life force. For them, the two were not inextricably intertwined; they were joined only circumstantially.

Those sorcerers affirmed that the *dark sea of awareness* doesn't want to take the lives of human beings; it wants only their life experiences. Lack of discipline in human beings prevents them from separating the two forces, and in the end, they lose their lives, when it is meant that they lose only the force of their life experiences. Those sorcerers viewed the *recapitulation* as the procedure by which they could give the *dark sea of awareness* a substitute for their lives. They gave up their life experiences by recounting them, but they retained their life force.

The perceptual claims of sorcerers, when examined in terms of the linear concepts of our Western world, make no sense whatsoever. Western civilization has been in contact with the shamans of the New World for five hundred years, and there has never been a genuine attempt on the part of scholars to formulate a serious philosophical discourse based on statements made by those shamans. For instance, the *recapitulation* may seem to any member of the Western world to be congruous with psychoanalysis, something in the line of a psychological procedure, a sort of self-help technique. Nothing could be further from the truth.

According to don Juan Matus, man always loses by default. In the case of the premises of sorcery, he believed that Western man is missing a tremendous opportunity for the enhancement of his awareness, and that the way in which Western man relates himself to the universe, life, and awareness is only one of a multiplicity of options.

To *recapitulate*, for shaman practitioners, means to give to an incomprehensible force—the *dark sea of awareness*—the very thing it seems to be looking for: their life experiences, that is to say, the awareness that they have enhanced through those very life experiences. Since don Juan could not possibly explain these phenomena to me in terms of standard logic, he said that all that sorcerers could aspire to do was to accomplish the feat of retaining their life force without knowing how it was done. He also said that there were thousands of sorcerers who had achieved this. They had retained their life force after they had given the *dark sea of awareness* the force of their life experiences. This meant to don Juan that those sorcerers didn't die in the usual sense in which we understand death, but that they transcended it by retaining their life force and vanishing from the face of the earth, embarked on a *definitive journey* of perception.

The belief of the shamans of don Juan's lineage was that when death takes place in this fashion, all of our being is turned into energy, a special kind of energy that retains the mark of our individuality. Don Juan tried to explain this in a metaphorical sense, saying that we are composed of a number of *single nations:* the nation of the lungs, the nation of the heart, the nation of the stomach, the nation of the kidneys, and so on. Each of these nations sometimes works independently of the others, but at the moment of death, all of them are unified into one single entity. The sorcerers of don Juan's lineage called this state *total freedom.* For those sorcerers, death is a unifier, and not an annihilator, as it is for the average man.

"Is this state immortality, don Juan?" I asked.

"This is in no way immortality," he replied. "It is merely the entrance into an evolutionary process, using the only medium for evolution that man has at his disposal: awareness. The sorcerers of my lineage were convinced that man could not evolve biologically any further; therefore, they considered man's awareness to be the only medium for evolution. At the moment of dying, sorcerers are not annihilated by death, but are transformed into *inorganic beings:* beings that have awareness, but not an organism. To be transformed into an inorganic being was evolution for them, and it meant that a new, indescribable type of awareness was lent to them, an awareness that would last for veritably millions of years, but which would also someday have to be returned to the giver: the *dark sea of awareness.*"

One of the most important findings of the shamans of don Juan's lineage was that, like everything else in the universe, our world is a combination of two opposing, and at the same time complementary, forces. One of those forces is the world we know, which those sorcerers called *the world of organic beings.* The other force is something they called *the world of inorganic beings.*

"The world of inorganic beings," don Juan said, "is populated by beings that possess awareness, but not an organism. They are conglomerates of energy fields, just like we are. To the eye of a seer, instead of being luminous, as human beings are, they are rather opaque. They are not round, but long, candlelike energetic configurations. They are, in essence, conglomerates of energy fields which have cohesion and boundaries just like we do. They are held together by the same agglutinating force that holds our energy fields together."

"Where is this inorganic world, don Juan?" I asked.

"It is our twin world," he replied. "It occupies the same time and space as our world, but the type of awareness of our world is so different from the type of awareness of the inorganic world that we never notice the presence of inorganic beings, although they do notice ours."

"Are those inorganic beings human beings that have evolved?" I asked.

"Not at all!" he exclaimed. "The inorganic beings of our twin world have been intrinsically inorganic from the start, the same way that we have always been intrinsically organic beings, also from the start. They are beings whose consciousness can evolve just like ours, and it doubtlessly does, but I have no firsthand knowledge of how this happens. What I do know, however, is that a human being whose awareness has evolved is a bright, luminescent, round inorganic being of a special kind."

Don Juan gave me a series of descriptions of this evolutionary process, which I always took to be poetic metaphors. I singled out the one that pleased me the most, which was *total freedom*. I fancied a human being that enters into *total freedom* to be the most courageous, the most imaginative being possible. Don Juan said that I was not fancying anything at all—that to enter into *total freedom*, a human being must call on his or her sublime side, which, he said, human beings have, but which it never occurs to them to use.

Don Juan described the second, the pragmatic goal of the *recapitulation* as the *acquisition of fluidity*. The sorcerers' rationale behind this had to do with one of the most elusive subjects of sorcery: the *assemblage point*, a point of intense luminosity the size of a tennis ball, perceivable when sorcerers *see* a human being as a conglomerate of energy fields.

Sorcerers like don Juan *see* that trillions of energy fields in the form of filaments of light from the universe at large converge on the *assemblage point* and go through it. This confluence of filaments gives the *assemblage point* its brilliancy. The *assemblage point* makes it possible for a human being to perceive those trillions of energy filaments by turning them into sensorial data. The *assemblage point* then interprets this data as the world of everyday life, that is to say, in terms of human socialization and human potential.

To *recapitulate* is to relive every, or nearly every, experience that we have had, and in doing so to displace the *assemblage point*, ever so slightly or a great deal, propelling it by the force of memory to adopt the position that it had when the event being *recapitulated* took place. This act of going back and forth from previous positions to the current one gives the shaman practitioners the necessary fluidity to withstand extraordinary odds in their journeys into *infinity*. To the Tensegrity practitioners, the *recapitulation* gives the necessary fluidity to withstand odds which are not in any way part of their habitual cognition.

The *recapitulation* as a formal procedure was done in ancient times by recollecting every person the practitioners knew and every experience in which they had taken part. Don Juan suggested that in my case, which is the case of modern man, I make a written list of all the persons that I had met in my life, as a mnemonic device. Once I had written that list, he proceeded to tell me how to use it. I had to take the first person on the list, which went backwards in time from the present to the time of my very first life experience, and set up, in my memory, my last interaction with that first person on my list. This act is called *arranging the event to be recapitulated.*

A detailed recollection of minutiae is required as the proper means to hone one's capacity to remember. This recollection entails getting all the pertinent physical details, such as the surroundings where the event being recollected took place. Once the event is arranged, one should enter into the locale itself, as if actually going into it, paying special attention to any relevant physical configurations. If, for instance, the interaction took place in an office, what should be remembered is the floor, the doors, the walls, the pictures, the windows, the desks, the objects on the desks, everything that could have been observed in a glance and then forgotten.

The *recapitulation* as a formal procedure must begin by the recounting of events that have just taken place. In this fashion, the primacy of the experience takes precedence. Something that has just happened is something that one can remember with great accuracy. Sorcerers always count on the fact that human beings are capable of storing detailed information that they are not aware of, and that that detail is what the *dark sea of awareness* is after.

The actual *recapitulation* of the event requires that one breathe deeply, fanning the head, so to speak, very slowly and gently from side to side, beginning on one side, left or right, whichever. This fanning of the head was done as many times as needed, while remembering all the details accessible. Don Juan said that sorcerers talked about this act as breathing in all of one's own feelings spent in the event being recollected, and expelling all the unwanted moods and extraneous feelings that were left with us.

Sorcerers believe that the mystery of the *recapitulation* lies in the act of inhaling and exhaling. Since breathing is a life-sustaining function, sorcerers are certain that by means of it, one can also deliver to the *dark sea of awareness* the facsimile of one's life experiences. When I pressed don Juan for a rational explanation of this idea, his position was that things like the *recapitulation* could only be experienced, not explained. He said that in the act of doing, one can find liberation, and that to explain it was to dissipate our energy in fruitless efforts. His invitation was congruous with everything related to his knowledge: the invitation to take action.

The list of names is used in the *recapitulation* as a mnemonic device that propels memory into an inconceivable journey. Sorcerers' position in this respect is that remembering events that have just taken place prepares the ground for remembering events more distant in time with the same clarity and immediacy. To recollect experiences in this way is to relive them, and to draw from this recollection an extraordinary impetus that is capable of stirring energy dispersed from our centers of vitality, and returning it to them. Sorcerers refer to this *redeployment of energy* that the *recapitulation* causes as gaining fluidity after giving the *dark sea of awareness* what it is looking for.

On a more mundane level, the *recapitulation* gives practitioners the capacity to examine the repetition in their lives. *Recapitulating* can convince them, beyond the shadow of a doubt, that all of us are at the mercy of forces which ultimately make no sense, although at first sight they seem perfectly reasonable; such as being at the mercy of courtship. It seems that for some people, courtship is the pursuit of a lifetime. I have personally heard from people of advanced age that the only ideal that they had was to find a perfect companion, and that their aspiration was to have perhaps one year of happiness in love.

Don Juan Matus used to say to me, over my vehement protests, that the problem was that nobody really wanted to love anybody, but that every one of us wanted to *be* loved. He said that this obsession with courtship, taken at face value, was the most natural thing in the world to us. To hear a seventy-five-year-old man or woman say that they are still in search of a perfect companion is an affirmation of something idealistic, romantic, beautiful. However, to examine this obsession in the context of the endless repetitions of a lifetime makes it appear as it really is: something grotesque.

Don Juan assured me that if any behavioral change is going to be accomplished, it has to be done through the *recapitulation*, since it is the only vehicle that can enhance awareness by liberating one from the unvoiced demands of socialization, which are so automatic, so taken for granted, that they are not even noticed under normal conditions, much less examined.

The actual act of *recapitulating* is a lifetime endeavor. It takes years to exhaust the list of people, especially for those who have made the acquaintance of and have interacted with thousands of individuals. This list is augmented by the memory of impersonal events in which no people are involved, but which have to be examined because they are somehow related to the person being *recapitulated*.

Don Juan asserted that what the sorcerers of ancient Mexico sought avidly in *recapitulating* was the memory of interaction, because in interaction lie the deep effects of socialization, which they struggled to overcome by any means available.

The Magical Passes for the Recapitulation

The *recapitulation* affects something that don Juan called the *energy body*. He formally explained the *energy body* as a conglomerate of energy fields that are the mirror image of the energy fields that make up the human body when it is *seen* directly as energy. He said that in the case of sorcerers, the physical body and the *energy body* are one single unit. The magical passes for the *recapitulation* bring the *energy body* to the physical body, which are essential for navigating into the unknown.

13. Forging the Trunk of the *Energy Body*

Don Juan said that the trunk of the *energy body* was forged with three strikes delivered with the palms of the hands. The hands are held at

Figure 152

the level of the ears with the palms facing forward, and from that position they strike forward, at the level of the shoulders, as if they were striking the shoulders of a well-developed body. The hands then move back to their original position around the ears, with the palms facing forward, and strike the midtrunk of that imaginary body at the level of the chest. The second strike is not as wide as the first one, and the third strike is much narrower, because it strikes the waistline of a triangular-shaped trunk (fig. 152).

14. Slapping the *Energy Body*

The left and the right hands each come down from above the head. The palm of each hand bears down, creating a current of energy that defines each arm, forearm, and hand of the *energy body*. The left hand hits across the body to strike the left hand of the *energy body* (fig. 153) and then the right hand does the same: it hits across the body to strike the right hand of the *energy body*.

This magical pass defines the arms and forearms, especially the hands, of the *energy body*.

15. Spreading the *Energy Body* Laterally

The wrists are crossed in the shape of a letter X in front of the body, almost touching it. The wrists are held bent backwards at a ninety-degree angle to the forearm, at the level of the solar plexus. The left wrist is on top of the right one (fig. 154). From there, the hands spread to the sides in unison, in a

Figure 153

slow motion, as if they met with tremendous resistance (fig. 155). When the arms reach their maximum aperture, they are brought back to the center, with the palms turned at a ninety-degree angle in relation to the forearms, creating in this fashion the sensation of pushing solid matter from both sides to the center of the body. The left hand crosses on top of the right as the hands get ready for another lateral strike.

While the physical body as a conglomerate of energy fields has super-defined boundaries, the *energy body* lacks that feature. Spreading energy laterally gives the *energy body* the defined boundaries that it lacks.

Figure 154

Figure 155

16. Establishing the Core of the *Energy Body*

The forearms are held in a vertical position at the level of the chest, with the elbows kept in close to the body, at the width of the trunk. The wrists are snapped back gently, and then forward with great force, without moving the forearms (fig. 156).

Figure 156

The human body, as a conglomerate of energy fields, has not only super-defined boundaries, but a core of compact luminosity, which shamans call *the band of man*, or the energy fields with which man is most familiar. The idea of shamans is that within the luminous sphere, which is also the totality of man's energetic possibilities, there are areas of energy of which human beings are not at all aware. Those are the energy fields located at the maximum distance from the *band of man*. To establish the core of the *energy body* is to fortify the *energy body* in order for it to venture into those areas of unknown energy.

17. Forging the Heels and the Calves of the *Energy Body*

The left foot is held in front of the body with the heel raised to midcalf. The heel is turned out to a position perpendicular to the other leg. Then the left heel strikes to the right as if a kick with the heel were

Figure 157

Figure 158

being delivered, about six or seven inches away from the shinbone of the right leg (figs. 157, 158).

The same movement is then executed with the other leg.

18. Forging the Knees of the *Energy Body*

This magical pass has two facets. In the first facet the left knee is bent and raised to the level of the hips, or if possible even higher. The total

Figure 159   *Figure 160*

weight of the body is placed on the right leg, which stands with the knee slightly bent forward. Three circles are drawn with the left knee, moving it inward toward the groin (fig. 159). The same movement is repeated with the right leg.

In the second facet of this magical pass, the movements are repeated again with each leg, but this time, the knee draws an outward circle (fig. 160).

19. Forging the Thighs of the *Energy Body*

Beginning with an exhalation, the body bends slightly at the knees as the hands slide down the thighs. The hands stop on top of the kneecaps, and then they are pulled back up the thighs to the level of the hips with an inhalation, as if they were dragging a solid substance. There is a slight quality of a

Figure 161

claw to each hand. The body straightens as this part of the movement is executed (fig. 161).

With the opposite breathing pattern, the movement is repeated, inhaling as the knees bend and the hands go down to the tops of the kneecaps, and exhaling as they are pulled back.

Figure 162

20. Stirring Up Personal History by Making It Flexible

This magical pass stretches the hamstring and relaxes it by bringing each leg, one at a time, bent at the knee, to strike the buttocks with a gentle tap of the heel (fig. 162). The left heel strikes the left buttock, and the right heel strikes the right one.

Shamans put an enormous emphasis on tightening the muscles of the backs of the thighs. They believe that the tighter those muscles, the greater the facility of the practitioner to identify and get rid of behavioral patterns that are useless.

21. Stirring Up Personal History with the Heel to the Ground by Tapping It Repeatedly

The right leg is set at a ninety-degree angle with the left. The left foot is placed as far as possible in front of the body as the body almost sits on the right leg. The tension and contraction of the back muscles of the right leg are maximum, as is the stretching of the back muscles of the left leg. The left leg taps the ground repeatedly with the heel (fig. 163).

The same movements are then executed with the other leg.

Figure 163

22. Stirring Up Personal History with the Heel to the Ground by Sustaining That Position

The same movements are executed in this magical pass as in the previous one, again with each leg, but instead of tapping with the heel, the body is kept at an even tension by holding the stretch of the leg (fig. 164).

The following four magical passes, since they entail deep inhalations and exhalations, have to be done sparingly.

Figure 164

23. The *Recapitulation* Wings
A deep inhalation is taken as both forearms are raised to the level of the shoulders, with the hands at the level of the ears, palms facing forward. The forearms are held vertically and equidistant from each other. An exhalation follows as the forearms are pulled back as far as possible without slanting them in any direction (fig. 165). Another deep inhalation is taken. Within the duration of one long exhalation, both arms each draw a winglike semicircle, beginning with the left arm moving forward as far as it can be extended and then laterally, drawing a semicircle to the back as far as possible. The arm makes a curve at the end of this extension and returns to the front (fig. 166) to its initial resting position by the side of the body (fig. 167). Then the right arm follows the same pattern within the same exhalation. Once these movements are completed, a deep abdominal breath is taken.

Figure 165　　　　*Figure 166*　　　　*Figure 167*

24. The Window of *Recapitulation*

The first part of this magical pass is exactly like the preceding one; a deep breath is taken with the hands raised to the ear level, with the palms facing forward. The forearms maintain a perfect verticality. This is followed by a long exhalation as the arms are pulled backwards. A deep inhalation is taken as the elbows are extended laterally at the level of the shoulders. The hands are bent at a ninety-degree angle in relation to the forearms, the fingers pointing upward. The hands are slowly pushed toward the center of the body until the forearms cross. The left arm is held closer to the body and the right arm is placed in front of the left. The hands create in this fashion what don Juan called the *window of recapitulation:* an opening in front of the eyes that looks like a small window, through which, don Juan affirmed, a practitioner could peer into *infinity* (fig. 168). A deep exhalation follows as the body straightens; the elbows are extended laterally and the hands are straightened out and kept at the same level as the elbows (fig. 169).

Figure 168   Figure 169

25. The Five Deep Breaths

The beginning of this magical pass is exactly like the previous two. At the second inhalation, the arms go down and cross at the level of the knees as the practitioner adopts a semi-squatting position. The hands are placed behind the knees; the right hand grabs the tendons in back of the left knee, and the left hand, with the left forearm on top of the right, grabs the tendons in back of the right knee. The index and middle fingers grab the outer tendons there and the thumb is wrapped around the inner part of the knee. The exhalation ends then, and a deep inhalation is taken, accompanied by pressing the tendon (fig. 170). Five breaths are taken in this fashion.

This magical pass causes the back to be straight and the head to be in alignment with the spine, and is used to take deep breaths that fill the top as well as the lower part of the lungs by pushing the diaphragm downward.

Figure 170

26. Drawing Energy from the Feet

The first part of this magical pass is exactly the same as the beginning of the other three of this series. On the second inhalation, the forearms go down and wrap around the ankles, going from the inside to the outside as the practitioner adopts a squatting position. The backs of the hands rest on top of the toes, and in this fashion, three deep inhalations and three deep exhalations are made (fig. 171). After the last exhalation, the body straightens as a deep inhalation is taken to finish the magical pass.

Figure 171

The only glow of awareness left in human beings is at the bottom of their luminous spheres, a fringe that extends in a circle and reaches the level of the toes. With this magical pass, that fringe is tapped with the backs of the fingers, and stirred with the breath.

The Third Group:

Dreaming

Don Juan Matus defined *dreaming* as the act of using normal dreams as a bona fide entrance for human awareness into other realms of perceiving. This definition implied for him that ordinary dreams could be used as a hatch that led perception into other regions of energy different from the energy of the world of everyday life, and yet utterly similar to it at a basic core. The result of such an entrance was, for sorcerers, the perception of veritable worlds where they could live or die, worlds which were astoundingly different from ours, and yet utterly similar.

Pressed for a linear explanation of this contradiction, don Juan Matus reiterated the standard position of sorcerers: that the answers to all those questions were in the practice, not in the intellectual inquiry. He said that in order to talk about such possibilities, we would have to use the syntax of language, whatever language we spoke, and that syntax, by the force of usage, limits the possibilities of expression. The syntax of any language refers only to perceptual possibilities found in the world in which we live.

Don Juan made a significant differentiation, in Spanish, between two verbs: one was to dream, *soñar*; and the other was *ensoñar*, which is to *dream* the way sorcerers *dream*. In English, there is no clear distinction between these two states: the normal dreaming, *sueño*, and the more complex state that sorcerers call *ensueño*.

The art of *dreaming*, according to what don Juan taught, originated in a very casual observation that the shamans of ancient Mexico made when they *saw* people who were asleep. They noticed that during sleep the *assemblage point* was displaced in a very natural, easy way from its habitual position, and that it moved anywhere along the periphery of the luminous sphere, or to any place in the interior of it. Correlating their *seeing* with the reports of the people who had been observed sleeping, they realized that the greater the observed displacement of the *assemblage point*, the more astounding the reports of events and scenes experienced in dreams.

After this observation took hold of them, those sorcerers began to look avidly for opportunities to displace their own *assemblage points*. They ended up using psychotropic plants to accomplish this. Very quickly, they realized that the displacement brought about by using these plants was erratic, forced, and out of control. In the midst of this failure, nonetheless they discovered one thing of great value. They called it *dreaming attention*.

Don Juan explained this phenomenon, referring first to the daily awareness of human beings as the *attention* placed on the elements of the world of everyday life. He pointed out that human beings took only a cursory and yet sustained look at everything that surrounded them.

More than examining things, human beings simply established the presence of those elements by a special type of *attention*, a specific aspect of their general awareness. His contention was that the same type of cursory and yet sustained "look," so to speak, could be applied to the elements of an ordinary dream. He called this other, specific aspect of general awareness *dreaming attention* or the capacity that practitioners acquire to maintain their awareness unwaveringly fixed on the items of their dreams.

The cultivation of *dreaming attention* gave the sorcerers of don Juan's lineage a basic taxonomy of dreams. They found out that most of their dreams were imagery, products of the cognition of their daily world; however, there were some which escaped that classification. Such dreams were veritable states of *heightened awareness* in which the elements of the dream were not mere imagery, but energy-generating affairs. Dreams which had energy-generating elements were, for those shamans, dreams in which they were capable of *seeing* energy as it flowed in the universe.

Those shamans were able to focus their *dreaming attention* on any element of their dreams, and found out, in this fashion, that there are two kinds of dreams. One is the dreams that we are all familiar with, in which phantasmagorical elements come into play, something which we could categorize as the product of our mentality, our psyche; perhaps something that has to do with our neurological makeup. The other kind of dreams they called *energy-generating dreams*. Don Juan said that those sorcerers of ancient times found themselves in dreams which were not dreams, but actual visitations made in a dreamlike state to bona fide places other than this world—real places, just like the world in which we live; places where the objects of the dream generated energy, just as trees, or animals, or even rocks generate energy in our daily world, for a *seeing* sorcerer.

Their visions of such places were, however, for those shamans, too fleeting, too temporary, to be of any value to them. They attributed this flaw to the fact that their *assemblage points* could not be held fixed for any considerable time at the position to which they had been displaced. Their attempts to remedy the situation resulted in the other high art of sorcery: the art of *stalking*.

Don Juan defined the two arts very clearly one day when he said to me that the art of *dreaming* consisted of purposely displacing the *assem-*

blage point from its habitual position. The art of *stalking* consisted in volitionally making it stay fixed on the new position to which it had been displaced.

This fixation allowed the shamans of ancient Mexico the opportunity to witness other worlds in their full extent. Don Juan said that some of those sorcerers never returned from their journeys. In other words, they opted for staying there, wherever "there" might have been.

"When the old sorcerers finished mapping human beings as luminous spheres," don Juan said to me once, "they had discovered no less than six hundred spots in the total luminous sphere that were the sites of bona fide worlds. Meaning that, if the *assemblage point* became attached to any of those places, the result was the entrance of the practitioner into a total new world."

"But where are those six hundred other worlds, don Juan?" I asked.

"The only answer to that question is incomprehensible," he said, laughing. "It's the essence of sorcery, and yet it means nothing to the average mind. Those six hundred worlds are in the position of the *assemblage point*. Incalculable amounts of energy are required to make sense out of this answer. We have the energy. What we lack is the facility or disposition to use it."

I could add that nothing could be truer than all these statements, and yet, nothing could make less sense.

Don Juan explained usual perception in the terms in which the sorcerers of his lineage understood it: The *assemblage point*, at its habitual location, receives an inflow of energy fields from the universe at large in the form of luminous filaments, numbering in the trillions. Since its position is consistently the same, it stood to sorcerers' reasoning that the same energy fields, in the form of luminous filaments, converge on the *assemblage point* and go through it, giving as a consistent result the perception of the world that we know. Those sorcerers arrived at the unavoidable conclusion that if the *assemblage point* were displaced to another position, another set of energy filaments would go through it, resulting in the perception of a world that, by definition, was not the same as the world of everyday life.

In don Juan's opinion, what human beings ordinarily regard as perceiving is rather the act of interpreting sensory data. He maintained that from the moment of birth, everything around us supplies us with a possibility of interpretation, and that with time, this possibility turns into a full system by means of which we conduct all of our perceptual transactions in the world.

He pointed out that the *assemblage point* is not only the center where perception is assembled, but also the center where the interpretation of sensory data is accomplished, so that if it were to change locations, it would interpret the new influx of energy fields in very much the same terms in which it interprets the world of everyday life. The result of this new interpretation is the perception of a world which is strangely similar to ours, and yet intrinsically different. Don Juan said that energetically, those other worlds are as different from ours as they could possibly be. It is only the interpretation of the *assemblage point* which accounts for the seeming similarities.

Don Juan called for a new syntax that could be used in order to express this wondrous quality of the *assemblage point* and the possibilities of perception brought about by *dreaming*. He conceded, however, that perhaps the present syntax of our language could be forced to cover it if this experience became available to any one of us, and not merely to shaman initiates.

Something related to *dreaming* that was of tremendous interest to me, but which bewildered me to no end, was don Juan's statement that there was really no procedure to speak of that would teach anyone how to *dream*. He said that more than anything else, *dreaming* was an arduous effort on the part of the practitioners to put themselves in contact with the indescribable all-pervading force that the sorcerers of ancient Mexico called *intent*. Once this link was established, *dreaming* also mysteriously became established. Don Juan asserted that this linkage could be accomplished following any pattern that implied discipline.

When I asked him to give me a succinct explanation of the procedures involved, he laughed at me.

"To venture into the world of sorcerers," he said, "is not like learning to drive a car. To drive a car, you need manuals and instructions. To *dream*, you need to *intend* it."

"But how can I *intend* it?" I insisted.

"The only way you could *intend* it is by *intending* it," he declared. "One of the most difficult things for a man of our day to accept is a lack of procedure. Modern man is in the throes of manuals, praxes, methods, steps leading to. He is ceaselessly taking notes, making diagrams, deeply involved in the 'know-how.' But in the world of sorcerers, procedures and rituals are mere designs to attract and focus attention. They are devices used to force a focusing of interest and determination. They have no other value."

What don Juan considered to be of supreme importance in order to *dream* is the rigorous execution of the magical passes: the only device that the sorcerers of his lineage used to aid the displacement of the *assemblage point*. The execution of the magical passes gave those sorcerers the stability and the energy necessary to call forth their *dreaming attention*, without which there was no possibility of *dreaming* for them. Without the emergence of *dreaming attention*, practitioners could aspire, at best, to have lucid dreams about phantasmagorical worlds. They could perhaps have views of worlds that generate energy, but these would make no sense to them whatsoever in the absence of an all-inclusive rationale that would properly categorize them.

Once the shamans of don Juan's lineage had developed their *dreaming attention*, they realized that they had tapped on the *doors of infinity*. They had succeeded in enlarging the parameters of their normal perception. They discovered that their normal state of awareness was infinitely more varied than it had been before the advent of their *dreaming attention*. From that point on, those sorcerers could truthfully venture into the unknown.

"The aphorism," don Juan said to me once, "that 'the sky is the limit' was most applicable to the sorcerers of ancient times. They certainly outdid themselves."

"Was it really true for them that the sky was the limit, don Juan?" I asked.

"This question could be answered only by each of us individually," he said, smiling expansively. "They gave us the tools. It is up to us individually to use them or refuse them. In essence, we are alone in front of *infinity*, and the issue of whether or not we are capable of reaching our limits has to be answered personally."

The Magical Passes for Dreaming

27. Getting the *Assemblage Point* Loose

The left arm, with the palm of the hand turned upward, reaches over the area behind the shoulder blades, as the trunk leans a bit forward. Then the arm is brought in an underhanded motion from the left side of the body to the front, moving in an upward thrust in front of the face, with the palm of the left hand turned to face the left. The fingers are held together (figs. 172, 173).

This magical pass is executed by each arm in succession. The knees are kept bent for greater stability and thrusting force.

Figure 172

Figure 173

28. Forcing the *Assemblage Point* to Drop Down

The back is kept as straight as possible. The knees are locked. The left arm, fully stretched, is placed at the back, a few inches away from the body. The hand is bent at a ninety-degree angle in relation to the forearm; the palm faces downward and the fully stretched fingers point backward. The fully stretched right arm is placed in front in the same position: with the wrist bent at a ninety-degree angle, the palm facing downward, the fingers pointing forward.

The head turns in the direction of the arm that is kept at the back, and a total stretch of the tendons of the legs and arms takes place at that instant. This tension of the tendons is held for a moment (fig. 174). The same movement is repeated with the right arm in back and the left in front.

Figure 174

29. Enticing the *Assemblage Point* to Drop by Drawing Energy from the Adrenals and Transferring It to the Front

The left arm is placed behind the body at the level of the kidneys, as far to the right as it can reach; the hand is held like a claw. The clawed hand moves across the kidney area from right to left as if dragging a solid substance. The right arm is held in its normal position by the side of the thigh.

Next, the left hand moves to the front; the palm is held flat, on the right side, against the liver and gallbladder. The left hand moves across the front of the body to the left, the area of the pancreas and spleen, as if smoothing the surface of a solid substance; at the same time the right hand, held like a claw behind the body, moves from left to right over the kidneys as if dragging a solid substance.

Then the right hand is placed on the front of the body; the palm is held flat against the area of the pancreas and spleen. The hand moves across the front of the body to the area of the liver and gallbladder, as if smoothing a rough surface, while the clawed left hand moves again across the area of the kidneys from right to left as if dragging a solid substance (figs. 175, 176). The knees are kept bent for greater stability and force.

Figure 175   Figure 176

30. Playing Out the A and B Types of Energy

The right forearm, bent in a vertical position, at a ninety-degree angle, is centered in front of the body, with the elbow almost at the level of the shoulders, and the palm of the hand facing left. The left forearm, bent at the elbow and held in a horizontal position, is placed with the back of the hand underneath the right elbow. The eyes, without focusing on either forearm, keep a peripheral view of both of them. The pressure of the right arm is downward, while the pressure of the left arm is upward. The two forces act simultaneously on both arms; they are kept under this tension for a moment (fig. 177).

Figure 177

Then the same movement is executed by reversing the order and position of the arms.

The shamans of ancient Mexico believed that everything in the universe is composed of dual forces, and that human beings are subjected to that duality in every aspect of their lives. At the level of energy, they considered that two forces are at play. Don Juan called them the *A and B forces*. The A force is employed ordinarily in our daily affairs, and is represented by a straight vertical line. The B force is ordinarily an obscure one which rarely enters into action, and it is kept lying down. It is represented by a horizontal line drawn to the left of the vertical one, at its base, making in this fashion a reversed capital letter L.

Shamans, men and women, were the only ones who, in don Juan's view, had been capable of turning the force B, which is ordinarily lying down horizontally, out of use, into an active vertical line. And consequently, they had succeeded in putting force A to rest. This process was represented by drawing a horizontal line at the base of the vertical one, to its right, and making, as a result, a capital letter L. Don Juan portrayed this magical pass as the one which best exemplified this duality and the effort of the sorcerers to reverse its effects.

31. Pulling the *Energy Body* to the Front

The arms are kept at shoulder level with the elbows bent. The hands overlap each other, and they are turned with the palms down. A circle is made with the hands rotating around each other; the movement is inward, toward the face (fig. 178). They rotate three times around each other; then the left arm is thrust forward with the hand in a fist, as if to strike an invisible target in front of the body, an arm's length away from it (fig. 179). Three more circles are drawn with both hands, and then the right arm strikes in the same fashion as the left one.

Figure 178   Figure 179

32. Hurling the *Assemblage Point* Like a Knife over the Shoulder

The left hand reaches over the head to the area behind the shoulder blades and grabs, as if holding a solid object. Then it moves over the head to the front of the body, with the motion of hurling something forward. The knees are kept bent for hurling stability. The same movement is repeated with the right arm (figs. 180, 181).

Figure 180   Figure 181

This magical pass is an actual attempt to hurl the *assemblage point*, in order to displace it from its habitual position. The practitioner holds the *assemblage point* as if it were a knife. Something in the *intent* of hurling the *assemblage point* causes a profound effect toward the actual displacement of it.

33. Hurling the *Assemblage Point* Like a Knife from the Back by the Waist

The knees are kept bent as the body leans forward. Then the left arm reaches to the back, from the side, to the area behind the shoulder blades, grabs onto something as if it were solid, and hurls it forward from the waist, with a flick of the wrist, as if hurling a flat disk, or a knife (figs. 182, 183). The same movements are repeated with the right hand.

Figure 182   Figure 183

34. Hurling the *Assemblage Point* Like a Disk from the Shoulder

A deep rotation of the waist is made to the left, which propels the right arm to swing to the left side of the left leg. Then the motion of the waist, moving in the opposite direction, propels the left arm to swing to the right side of the right leg. Another motion of the waist propels the right arm to swing again to the left side of the left leg. At this point the left hand reaches back instantly with a circular motion to grab onto something as if it were solid, from the area behind the shoulder blades (fig. 184). The left hand takes it in a swinging circular motion to the front of the body and up to the level of the right shoulder. The palm of the clenched hand faces upward. From this position, the left hand, with a flick of the wrist, makes a hurling motion, as if to hurl forward something solid, like a disk (fig. 185).

The legs are kept bent slightly at the knees and a great pressure is exerted at the back of the thighs. The right arm, with the elbow slightly bent, is extended behind the body to give stability to the act of hurling a disk. This position is held for a moment, while the left arm maintains the position of having just hurled an object.

The same movements are repeated with the other arm.

Figure 184

Figure 185

Figure 186

35. Hurling the *Assemblage Point* Like a Ball Above the Head

The left hand moves back quickly to the area behind the shoulder blades and grabs something, as if it were solid (fig. 186). The arm rotates twice in a big circle above the head as if to gain impulse (fig. 187) and makes the motion of hurling a ball forward (fig. 188). The knees are kept bent. These movements are repeated with the right hand.

Figure 187   Figure 188

The Fourth Group:
Inner Silence

Don Juan said that *inner silence* was the state most avidly sought by the shamans of ancient Mexico. He defined it as a natural state of human perception in which thoughts are blocked off and all of man's faculties operate from a level of awareness which doesn't require the utilization of our daily cognitive system.

Inner silence has always been associated with darkness, for the shamans of don Juan's lineage, perhaps because human perception, deprived of its habitual companion, the *internal dialogue*, falls into something that resembles a dark pit. He said that the body functions as usual, but awareness becomes sharper. Decisions are instantaneous, and seem to stem from a special sort of knowledge which is deprived of thought-verbalizations.

Human perception functioning in a condition of *inner silence*, according to don Juan, is capable of reaching indescribable levels. Some of those levels of perception are worlds in themselves, and not at all like the worlds reached through *dreaming*. They are indescribable states, inexplicable in terms of the linear paradigms that the habitual state of human perception employs for explaining the universe.

Inner silence, in don Juan's understanding, is the matrix for a gigantic step of evolution: *silent knowledge,* or the level of human awareness where knowing is automatic and instantaneous. Knowledge at this level is not the product of cerebral cogitation or logical induction and deduction, or of generalizations based on similarities and dissimilarities. There is nothing a priori at the level of *silent knowledge,* nothing that could constitute a body of knowledge, for everything is imminently *now.* Complex pieces of information could be grasped without any cognitive preliminaries.

Don Juan believed that *silent knowledge* was insinuated to early man, but that early man was not really the possessor of *silent knowledge.* Such an insinuation was infinitely stronger than what modern man experiences, where the bulk of knowledge is the product of rote learning. It is a sorcerers' axiom that although we have lost that insinuation, the avenue that leads to *silent knowledge* will always be open to man by means of *inner silence.*

Don Juan Matus taught the hard line of his lineage: that *inner silence* must be gained by a consistent pressure of discipline. It has to be accrued or stored, bit by bit, second by second. In other words, one has to force oneself to be silent, even if it is only for a few seconds. According to don Juan, it was common knowledge among sorcerers that if one persists in this, persistence overcomes habit, and thus, it is possible to arrive at a threshold of accrued seconds or minutes, which differs from person to person. If the threshold of *inner silence* is ten minutes for a given individual, for instance, then once this threshold is reached, *inner silence* happens by itself, of its own accord, so to speak.

I was warned beforehand that there was no possible way of knowing what my individual threshold might be, and that the only way of finding this out was through direct experience. This is exactly what happened to me. Following don Juan's suggestion, I had persisted in forcing myself to remain silent, and one day, while walking at UCLA, I reached my mysterious threshold. I knew I had reached it because in one instant, I experienced something don Juan had described at length to me. He had called it *stopping the world.* In the blink of an eye, the world ceased to be what it was, and for the first time in my life, I became conscious that I was *seeing* energy as it flowed in the universe. I had to sit down on some brick steps. I knew that I was sitting on some brick steps, but I knew it only intellectually, through memory. Experientially, I was resting on energy. I myself was energy, and so was everything around me. I had canceled out my interpretation system.

After *seeing* energy directly, I realized something which became the horror of my day, something that no one could explain to me satisfactorily except don Juan. I became conscious that although I was *seeing* for the first time in my life, I had been *seeing* energy as it flows in the universe all my life, but I had not been conscious of it. To *see* energy as it flows in the universe was not the novelty. The novelty was the query that arose with such fury that it made me surface back into the world of everyday life. I asked myself what had been keeping me from realizing that I had been *seeing* energy as it flows in the universe all my life.

"There are two issues at stake here," don Juan explained to me, when I asked him about this maddening contradiction. "One is general awareness. The other is particular, deliberate consciousness. Every human being in the world is aware, in general terms, of *seeing* energy as it flows in the universe. However, only sorcerers are particularly and deliberately conscious of it. To become conscious of something that you are generally aware of requires energy, and the iron-hand discipline needed to get it. Your *inner silence,* the product of discipline and energy, bridged the gap between general awareness and particular consciousness."

Don Juan stressed, in every way he was able, the value of a pragmatic attitude in order to buttress the advent of *inner silence.* He defined a pragmatic attitude as the capacity to absorb any contingency that might appear along the way. He himself was, to me, the living example of such an attitude. There wasn't any uncertainty or liability that his mere presence would not dispel.

He reiterated every time he could that the effects of *inner silence* were very unsettling, and that the only deterrent to this condition was the pragmatic attitude which was the product of a superbly pliable, agile, strong body. He said that for sorcerers, the physical body was the only entity that made any sense to them, and that there was no such thing as a dualism between body and mind. He further stated that the physical body involved both the body and the mind as we knew them, and that in order to counterbalance the physical body as a holistic unit, sorcerers considered another configuration of energy which was reached through *inner silence:* the *energy body.* He explained that what I had experienced at the moment in which I had *stopped the world* was the resurgence of my *energy body,* and that this configuration of energy was the one which had always been able to *see* energy as it flowed in the universe.

THE MAGICAL PASSES THAT AID THE ATTAINMENT OF INNER SILENCE

Figure 189

36. Drawing Two Half-Circles with Each Foot

The total weight of the body is on the right leg. The left foot is placed half a step in front of it, and it slides on the floor, drawing a half-circle to the left; the ball of the foot comes to rest almost touching the right heel. From there, it draws another half-circle to the back (fig. 189). These circles are drawn with the ball of the left foot. The heel is kept off the ground, in order to make the movement smooth and uniform.

The movement is reversed and two more half-circles are drawn in this fashion, starting from the back and going to the front.

The same movements are executed with the right foot after the whole weight of the body is transferred to the left leg. The knee of the leg that supports the weight is bent for strength and stability.

Figure 190

37. Drawing a Half-Moon with Each Foot

The weight of the body is placed on the right leg. The left foot goes half a step in front of the right one, drawing a wide semicircle on the ground around the body from the front, to the left, to the back of the body. This semicircle is drawn with the ball of the foot (fig. 190). Another semicircle is drawn from the back to the front, in the same fashion. The same movements are executed with the right leg, after transferring the weight to the left leg.

38. The Scarecrow in the Wind with the Arms Down

The arms are kept extended laterally at the level of the shoulders with the elbows bent and the forearms dangling downward at a strict ninety-degree angle. The forearms swing freely from side to side, as if moved by the wind alone. The forearms and the wrists are kept straight and vertical. The knees are locked (fig. 191).

Figure 191

39. The Scarecrow in the Wind with the Arms Up

Just as in the preceding magical pass, the arms are extended laterally at the level of the shoulders, except the forearms are turned upward, bent at a ninety-degree angle. The forearms and wrists are kept straight and vertical (fig. 192). Then they swing freely downward to the front (fig. 193) and upward again. The knees are locked.

Figure 192   *Figure 193*

40. Pushing Energy Backward with the Full Arm

The elbows are acutely bent and the forearms held tight against the sides of the body, as high as possible, with the hands held in fists (fig.

194). As an exhalation is made, the forearms are fully extended downward and backward as high as possible. The knees are locked, and the trunk bends slightly forward (fig. 195). As an inhalation is made, the arms are then brought forward to the original position by bending the elbows.

Then the breathing is reversed as this movement is repeated; instead of exhaling as the arms are pulled backwards, an inhalation is taken. An exhalation follows as the elbows are bent and the forearms are brought upward against the axilla.

Figure 194

Figure 195

Figure 196

41. Pivoting the Forearm

The arms are held in front of the body with the elbows bent and the forearms vertical. Each hand is bent at the wrist, resembling the head of a bird, which is at eye level, with the fingers pointing toward the face (fig. 196). Keeping the elbows vertical and straight, the wrists are flipped back and forth, pivoting on the forearms, making the fingers of the hands move from pointing at the face to pointing forward (fig. 197). The knees are kept bent for stability and strength.

Figure 197

42. Moving Energy in a Ripple

The knees are kept straight, and the trunk stoops over. Both arms are kept dangling at the sides. The left arm moves forward with three ripples of the hand, as if the hand were following the contour of a surface with three half-circles on it (fig. 198). Next, the hand cuts across the front of the body in a straight line from left to right, then from right to left (fig. 199), and moves backward at the side of the body with three more ripples, drawing in this fashion the thick shape of an inverted capital letter L—at least six inches thick.

The same movements are repeated with the right arm.

Figure 198

Figure 199

43. The T Energy of the Hands

The two forearms are held at right angles right in front of the solar plexus, making the shape of a letter T. The left hand is the horizontal bar of the letter T with the palm turned upward. The right hand is the vertical bar of the letter T with the palm turned downward (fig. 200).

Figure 200   Figure 201

Next, the hands turn back and forth at the same time with considerable force. The palm of the left hand is turned to face downward, and the

Figure 202

palm of the right hand is turned to face upward, both hands maintaining the same letter T shape (fig. 201).

These same movements are executed again, placing the right hand as the horizontal bar of the letter T and the left hand as the vertical one.

44. Pressing Energy with the Thumbs

The forearms, bent at the elbows, are held right in front of the body in a perfectly horizontal position, maintaining the width of the body. The fingers are curled in a loose fist, and the thumbs are held straight, cradled on the curled index fingers (figs. 202, 203). An intermittent pressure is exerted between the thumb and the index finger and the

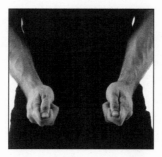

Figure 203

curled fingers against the palm of the hand. They contract and relax, spreading the impulse to the arms. The knees are kept bent for stability.

45. Drawing an Acute Angle with the Arms Between the Legs
The knees are locked, with the hamstrings as tight as possible. The trunk is bent forward, with the head almost at the level of the knees. The arms dangle in front and, moving repeatedly forward and backward, they draw an acute angle with its vertex between the legs (figs. 204, 205).

Figure 204

Figure 205

46. Drawing an Acute Angle with the Arms in Front of the Face
The knees are locked, with the hamstrings as tight as possible. The trunk is bent forward, with the head almost at the level of the knees. The arms dangle in front of the body and, moving repeatedly from the back to the front, they draw an acute angle, with its vertex in front of the face (figs. 206, 207).

Figure 206

Figure 207

47. Drawing a Circle of Energy Between the Legs and in Front of the Body

The knees are kept locked, with the hamstrings as tight as possible. The trunk is bent forward, with the head almost at the level of the knees. The arms dangle in front of the body. The two arms cross at the wrists, the left forearm on top of the right one. The crossed arms swing back between the legs (fig. 208). From there, each one makes an outward circle in front of the face. At the end of the circle, the arms point forward, the left wrist on top of the right one (fig. 209). From there, they draw

Figure 208

Figure 209

two inward circles that end between the legs, with the wrists crossed once more in the initial position.

Then the right wrist is made to rest on top of the left one, and the same movements are repeated.

48. Three Fingers on the Floor

The arms are brought slowly over the head as a deep inhalation is taken. A slow exhalation begins while the arms are brought all the way down to the floor, keeping the knees locked and the hamstrings as tight as possible. The index and middle fingers of each hand touch the floor a foot in front of the body, and then the thumb is also brought to rest on the floor (fig. 210). A deep inhalation is taken while that position is held. The body straightens, and the arms are raised above the head. The air is exhaled as the arms come down to the level of the waist.

Figure 210

49. The Knuckles on the Toes

The arms are raised above the head as a deep inhalation is taken. As the air is exhaled, the arms are brought all the way down to the floor, keeping the knees locked and the hamstrings as tight as possible. The knuckles are brought to rest on top of the toes as the exhalation ends (fig. 211). A deep inhalation is taken while that position is held. The body straightens, and the arms are raised above the head. The exhalation begins when the arms are brought down to the level of the waist.

Figure 211

50. Drawing Energy from the Floor with the Breath

A deep inhalation is taken as the arms are raised above the head; the knees are kept bent. The exhalation begins as the trunk turns to the left and bends down as far as possible. The hands, with the palms down, come to rest around the left foot, with the right hand in front of the foot and the left hand behind it; they move back and forth five times as the exhalation ends (fig. 212). A deep inhalation is taken then, and the body straightens as the arms move over the head. The trunk turns to

Figure 212

the right, and the exhalation begins as the trunk bends down as far as possible. The exhalation ends after the hands move back and forth five times by the right foot. Another deep breath is taken, and the body straightens up as the arms move above the head and the trunk pivots to face the front; then the arms come down as the air is exhaled.

The Separation of the Left Body and the Right Body: The Heat Series

Don Juan taught his disciples that for the shamans who lived in Mexico in ancient times, the concept that a human being is composed of two complete functioning bodies, one on the left and one on the right, was fundamental to their endeavors as sorcerers. Such a classificatory scheme had nothing to do with intellectual speculations on the part of those sorcerers, or with logical conclusions about possibilities of distribution of mass in the body.

When don Juan explained this to me, I countered that modern biologists had the concept of *bilateral symmetry*, which means "a basic body plan in which the left and right sides of the organism can be divided into approximate mirror images of each other along the midline."

"The classifications of the shamans of ancient Mexico," don Juan replied, "were more profound than the conclusions of modern scientists, because they stemmed from perceiving energy directly as it flows in the universe. When the human body is perceived as energy, it is utterly patent that it is composed not of two parts, but of two different types of energy: two different currents of energy, two opposing and at the same time complementary forces that coexist side by side, mirroring, in this fashion, the dual structure of everything in the universe at large."

The shamans of ancient Mexico accorded each·one of these two different kinds of energy the stature of a total body, and spoke exclusively in terms of the left body and the right body. Their emphasis was on the left body, because they considered it to be the most effective, in terms of the nature of its energy configuration, for the ultimate goals of shamanism. The shamans of ancient Mexico, who depicted the two bodies as streams of energy, depicted the left stream as being more turbulent and aggressive, moving in undulating ripples and projecting out waves of energy. When illustrating what he was talking about, don Juan asked me to visualize a scene in which the left body was like half of the sun, and that all the solar flares happened on that half. The waves of energy projected out of the left body were like those solar flares—always perpendicular to the round surface from which they originated.

He depicted the stream of energy of the right body as not being turbulent at all on the surface. It moved like water inside a tank which was being slightly tilted back and forth. There were no ripples in it, but a continuous rocking motion. At a deeper level, however, it swirled in rotational circles in the form of spirals. Don Juan asked me to envision a very wide, peaceful-looking tropical river, where the water on the surface seemed barely to move, but which had shattering riptides below the surface. In the world of everyday life, these two currents are amalgamated into a single unit: the human body as we know it.

To the eye of the seer, however, the energy of the total body is circular. This meant to the sorcerers of don Juan's lineage that the right body was the predominant force.

"What happens in the case of left-handed people?" I asked him once. "Are they more suitable for the endeavors of sorcerers?"

"Why do you think they should be?" he replied, seemingly surprised by my question.

"Because obviously, the left side is predominant," I said.

"This predominance is of no importance whatsoever for sorcerers," he said. "Yes, the left side predominates in the sense that they can hold a hammer with their left hand very effectively. They write with their left hand. They can hold a knife with their left hand, and do it very well. If they are leg shakers, they can certainly shake the left knee with great rhythm. In other words, they have rhythm in their left body, but sorcery is not a matter of that kind of predominance. The right body still rules them with a circular motion."

"But does left-handedness have any advantages or disadvantages for sorcerers?" I asked. I was driven by the implication built into many of the Indo-European languages of the sinister quality of left-handedness.

"There are no advantages or disadvantages to my knowledge," he said. "The division of energy between the two bodies is not measured by dexterity, or the lack of it. The predominance of the right body is an energetic predominance, which was encountered by the shamans of those ancient times. They never tried to explain why this predominance happened in the first place, nor did they try to further investigate the philosophical implications of it. For them, it was a fact, but a very special fact. It was a fact that could be changed."

"Why did they want to change it, don Juan?" I asked.

"Because the predominant circular motion of the right body's energy is too friggin' boring!" he exclaimed. "That circular motion certainly takes care of any event of the daily world, but it does it circularly, if you know what I mean."

"I don't know what you mean, don Juan," I said.

"Every situation in life is met in this circular fashion," he replied, making a small circle with his hand. "On and on and on and on and on. It's a circular movement that seems to draw the energy inward always, and turns it around and around in a centripetal motion. Under these conditions, there's no expansion. Nothing can be new. There is nothing that cannot be inwardly accounted for. What a drag!"

"In what way can this situation be changed, don Juan?" I asked.

"It's too late to be really changed," he replied. "The damage is already done. The spiral quality is here to remain. But it doesn't have to be ceaseless. Yes, we walk the way we do, we can't change that, but we would also like to run, or to walk backward, or to climb a ladder; just to walk and walk and walk and walk is very effective, but meaningless. The contribution of the left body would make those centers of vitality more pliable. If they could undulate instead of moving in spirals, if only for an instant, different energy would get into them, with staggering results."

I understood what he was talking about, at a level beyond thought, because there was really no way that I could have understood it linearly.

"The sensation that human beings have of being utterly bored with themselves," he continued, "is due to this predominance of the right body. The only thing left for human beings to do, in a universal sense, is to find ways of ridding themselves of boredom. What they end up doing is finding ways of killing time: the only commodity no one has enough of. But what's worse is the reaction to this unbalanced distribution of energy. The violent reactions of people are due to this unbalanced distribution. It seems that from time to time, helplessness builds furious currents of energy within the human body, which explode in violent behavior. Violence seems to be, for human beings, another way of killing time."

"But why is it, don Juan, that the sorcerers of ancient Mexico never wanted to know *why* this situation happened?" I asked, bewildered. I found what I was feeling about this inward motion to be fascinating.

"They never tried to find out," he said, "because the instant they formulated the question, they knew the answer."

"So they knew why?" I asked.

"No, they didn't know why, but they knew how it happened. But that's another story."

He left me hanging there, but throughout the course of my association with him, he explained this seeming contradiction.

"Awareness is the only avenue that human beings have for evolution," he said to me once, "and something extraneous to us, something that has to do with the predatorial condition of the universe, has interrupted our possibility of evolving by taking possession of our awareness. Human beings have fallen prey to a predatorial force, which has imposed on them, for its own convenience, the passivity which is characteristic of the energy of the right body."

Don Juan described our evolutionary possibility as a journey that our awareness takes across something the shamans of ancient Mexico called the *dark sea of awareness:* something which they considered to be an actual feature of the universe, an incommensurable element that permeates the universe, like clouds of matter, or light.

Don Juan was convinced that the predominance of the right body in this unbalanced merging of the right and left bodies marks the interruption of our *journey of awareness.* What seems for us to be the natural dominance of one side over the other was, for the sorcerers of his lineage, an aberration, which they strove to correct.

Those shamans believed that in order to establish a harmonious division between the left and the right bodies, practitioners needed to enhance their awareness. Any enhancement of human awareness, however, had to be buttressed by the most exigent discipline. Otherwise, this enhancement, painfully accomplished, would turn into an obsession, resulting in anything from psychological aberration to energetic injury.

Don Juan Matus called the collection of magical passes which deal exclusively with the separation between the left body and the right body *The Heat Group:* the most crucial element in the training of the shamans of ancient Mexico. This was a nickname given to this collection of magical passes because it makes the energy of the right body a little more turbulent. Don Juan Matus used to joke about this phenomenon, saying that the movements for the left body put an enormous pressure on the right body, which has been accustomed from birth to ruling without opposition. The moment it is faced with opposition, it gets hot with anger. Don Juan urged all his disciples to practice the Heat Group assiduously, in order to use its aggressiveness to reinforce the weak left body.

In Tensegrity, this group is called *The Heat Series*, in order to make it more congruous with the aims of Tensegrity, which are extremely pragmatic on the one hand and extremely abstract on the other, such as the practical utilization of energy for well-being coupled with the abstract idea of how that energy is obtained. In all the magical passes of this series, it is recommended to adopt the division of left and right bodies, rather than left and right sides of the body. The end result of this observance would be to say that during the execution of these magical passes, the body that doesn't perform the movements is kept immobile. However, all its muscles should be engaged, not in activity, but in awareness. This immobility of the body that is not performing the movements should be extended to include its head; that is to say, to the opposite side of the head. Such immobility of half of the face and head is more difficult to attain, but it can be accomplished with practice.

The series is divided into four groups.

The First Group:
Stirring Energy on the Left Body and the Right Body

The first group comprises sixteen magical passes that stir the energy of the left body and the right body, each independently from the other. Each magical pass is performed with either the left arm or the right arm, and in some cases with both at the same time. The arms never go, however, beyond the vertical line that separates the two bodies.

1. Gathering Energy in a Ball from the Front of the Left and the Right Bodies and Breaking It with the Back of the Hand

With the palm of the hand slightly curved and facing the right, the left arm circles inward twice in front of the body (fig. 213). All the muscles of the arm are held tense as this circular motion is executed. Then the back of the hand strikes forcefully to the left as if breaking the top of a ball gathered with the movement of the arm (fig. 214).

Figure 213   Figure 214

The hand strikes a point an arm's length away from the body above the shoulders, at a forty-five-degree angle. While this strike is being executed, all the muscles are kept tense, including the muscles of the arms, a tension that permits controlling the strike. The impact is felt on the areas of the pancreas and spleen and the left kidney and adrenals.

The same movements are repeated on the right side, and the impact is felt on the areas of the liver and the right kidney and adrenals.

2. Gathering Energy of the Left and Right Bodies in a Circle Which Is Perforated with the Tips of the Fingers

The left forearm is held in front of the body, at a ninety-degree angle in relation to it. The wrist is kept straight. The palm of the hand faces to the right as the fingers point to the front. The thumb is kept locked. As in the previous magical pass, the forearm circles twice, going from the left up to the level of the shoulder and turning toward the center of the body (fig.

215). The elbow is then quickly pulled all the way back, and the circle drawn by the forearm is perforated by the tips of the fingers in a forward thrust (fig. 216). The elbow is moved all the way back once more in order to gain striking power, and then the hand shoots forward again.

The same sequence of movements is performed with the right arm.

Figure 215   Figure 216

3. Hoisting Left and Right Energy Upward

Both knees are slightly bent. The left knee is then raised to the level of the pancreas, fully bent, while the foot is held with the toes pointing to the ground. At the same time that this movement is performed, the left forearm shoots upward until it reaches a point at a forty-five-degree angle with the body; the elbow is kept tight against the body. Both the leg and the arm move in total synchronicity, jolting the midsection (fig. 217).

The same movements are repeated with the right leg and the right arm.

The tendency of energy is to sink, and it is of great importance to spread it upward to the midsection of the body. It is the belief of shamans that the left body is ruled by the area of the pancreas and spleen, and the right

Figure 217

body by the area of the liver and gallbladder. Shamans understand this process of hoisting energy as a maneuver to energize those two centers separately.

4. The Up-and-Down Pressure

The left elbow is raised in front of the body to the level of the shoulder, bent at a ninety-degree angle with the forearm. The hand is clenched in a fist, and the wrist is bent toward the right as acutely as possible (fig. 218). Using the elbow as a pivot by keeping it at the same position, the forearm is bent downward until it reaches the area right in front of the solar plexus (fig. 219). The forearm then returns to the upright position.

The same movement is performed with the right arm.

This magical pass is used to stir up the energy that exists in an arc between a point just above the head and in line with the left shoulder and a point right above the solar plexus.

Figure 218   Figure 219

5. The Inward Turn

The first part of this magical pass is exactly like the first part of the preceding one, but instead of bending the forearm downward, it is made to rotate inwardly, making a complete circle, pivoting on the elbow at a forty-five-degree angle with the body. The top of the circle is at a point just above the ear and in line with the left shoulder. The wrist is also made to rotate as the circle is drawn (fig. 220).

The same movement is performed with the right hand.

Figure 220

6. The Outward Turn

This magical pass is almost identical to the preceding one, except that instead of turning the left forearm to the right to make a circle, it turns to the left (fig. 221). It makes what don Juan called an *outward circle*, as opposed to the circle made in the previous magical pass, which he called an *inward circle*.

The same movement is performed with the right hand.

In this magical pass, the energy stirred is part of the arc of energy dealt with in the two preceding magical passes. The fourth, fifth, and sixth magical passes of this group are performed together. Shamans have found out, by means of their *seeing*, that human beings have enormous caches of unused energy lying around inside their luminous spheres. They have also found out, in this manner, that these magical passes stir the energy dispersed from the respective centers of vitality—the one around the liver and the one around the pancreas—which stays suspended for quite a while before it begins to sink down to the bottom of the luminous sphere.

Figure 221

7. A High Push with the Fists

The arms are held in front of the body at the level of the shoulders. The hands are fisted with the palms turned toward the ground. The elbows

Figure 222

Figure 223

are bent. The left hand strikes forward with a short punch, without first retrieving the elbow to gain strength. The left hand is retrieved to its initial position; the right hand follows with another similar punch and is then retrieved to its original position (fig. 222). The strike of the fists comes from the contraction of the muscles of the arms, shoulder blades, and abdomen.

8. A Low Push with the Fists

The elbows are bent at a ninety-degree angle and kept at the level of the waist. They don't touch the body, but are kept an inch or two away from it. The hands are clenched in fists with the palms facing each other. The left forearm moves to strike in a short punch, driven by the muscles of the stomach, which contract in unison with the muscles of the arm and the shoulder blade (fig. 223). After striking, the forearm is retrieved instantly, as if the punch has generated the force to push the arm back. The right arm moves immediately afterward in the same fashion. Just as in the preceding pass, the elbows don't move back to gain striking strength; the strength is derived solely from the muscular tension of the abdomen, arms, and shoulder blades.

9. A Wheel with the Fingers Contracted at the Middle Joints

The elbows are kept at the level of the waist over the areas of the pancreas and spleen, and the liver and gallbladder. The wrists are kept straight; the palms of the hands face each other while the fingers are tightly clenched at the second knuckle. The thumbs are locked (fig. 224). The elbows move forward and away from the body. The left hand circles in a vertical rasping motion, as if the bent knuckles were rasping a surface in front of the body. Then the right hand does the same. The two hands move in an alternate fashion in such a manner (fig. 225). The muscles of the abdomen are kept as tight as possible in order to give impetus to this movement.

Figure 224   Figure 225

10. Smoothing Energy Out in Front of the Body

The flat palm of the left hand, which faces forward, is raised to a level just above the head, in front of the body. The palm slides downward in a slanted line and comes to the level of the pancreas and spleen, as if it were smoothing out a vertical surface. Without stopping there, it continues moving to the back; the body rotates to the left to allow the arm to come fully over the head. The hand, with the palm facing downward, then comes down with great force, as if to slap a rubbery substance in front of the area of the pancreas and spleen (fig. 226).

Exactly the same movements are performed with the right arm, but using the area of the liver and gallbladder as the striking point.

Figure 226

11. Hitting Energy in Front of the Face with an Upward Thrust of the Fist

The trunk turns slightly to the left in order to allow the left arm two full backward rotations going first to the front, above the head, then to the back, where the palm turns slightly inward as if to scoop something from the back (fig. 227). The movement ends at the second turn with an upward thrust of the fisted hand in front of the face (fig. 228).

Figure 227   Figure 228

This magical pass is repeated with the right arm in exactly the same sequence.

12. Hammering Energy in Front of the Left and Right Bodies

One and a half forward circles are made with the arm, followed by a downward strike; the body rotates slightly in order to allow the left arm a full rotation starting from its initial position by the side of the thigh to the back, above the head, to the front, and again to the side of the

Figure 229   Figure 230

thigh. As this circle is made, the palm is made to rotate at the wrist as if the hand were scooping up some viscous matter (fig. 229). From its initial position, the arm moves again to the back and above the head, where the hand turns into a fist that strikes down, with great force, at a point in front of and above the pancreas and spleen, using the soft edge of the hand like a hammer as the striking surface (fig. 230).

The same movements are repeated with the right arm.

13. Drawing Two Outward Circles of Energy and Smashing Them by the Navel

Both arms move in unison up the front of the body, out to the sides, and around, like a swimming stroke, to draw two winglike circles at forty-five-degree angles to the front of the body (fig. 231). Then the circles are broken at the bottom, at the level of the navel, with a forceful strike of both hands. The hands are bent at a ninety-degree angle in relation to the forearms, with the fingers pointing forward. The force of the strike makes the palms of the hands come within a few inches of each other (fig. 232).

Figure 231

Figure 232

14. Drawing Two Circles of Energy Laterally with the Index and Middle Fingers Extended

The index and middle fingers of both hands are fully extended, while the third and fourth fingers are held by the thumbs against the palms.

The arms circle in unison from their normal position at the sides to above the head and then laterally to the sides of the body at forty-five degree angles toward the back (fig. 233). When the full circle is nearly completed, the fingers contract into fists, leaving the second knuckles of the middle fingers protruding. The movement ends as the fists, with the palms facing the body, strike forward and upward, to the level of the chin (fig. 234).

Figure 233

Figure 234

15. Stirring the Energy Around the Temples

A long inhalation is taken. An exhalation begins as the arms are brought to a point above the head, where they clasp into fists; the palms of the fisted hands face the front of the body. From there they strike downward with a back-fist blow to a point right above the hips (fig. 235). The fisted hands move to the sides of the body, drawing lateral half-circles that bring the fists to an area a few inches in front of the forehead and five or six inches away from each other. The fisted palms face outward (fig. 236). While the exhalation still lasts, the fists are brought to rest on the temples for an instant. The body leans backward a bit by bending slightly at the knees to gain spring and momentum, and then the arms are brought forcefully down, without straightening the elbows, to strike behind the body on either side with the backs of the fisted hands (fig. 237). The exhalation ends there.

Figure 235

Figure 236

Figure 237

16. Projecting a Small Circle of Energy Out in Front of the Body

From its natural position by the side of the thigh, the left arm moves outward laterally; the palm of the hand faces the right. It draws a small circle as the palm turns downward, comes to the area of the pancreas and spleen, and continues moving left to the level of the waist. The elbow protrudes acutely (fig. 238a); the hand turns into a fist. The palm of the fisted hand faces the ground. The fist strikes with a short blow to

Figure 238a

Figure 238b

the front, as if to pierce the circle it has drawn (fig. 238b). The movement is continuous; it is not interrupted when the hand turns into a fist, but stops only when the punch has been delivered. The blow gives an intense jolt to the center of vitality located around the pancreas and spleen. The same movement is executed with the right hand, the strike of which jolts the liver and gallbladder.

The Second Group:
Mixing Energy from the Left Body
and the Right Body

The second group consists of fourteen magical passes that mix the energy of both bodies at their respective centers of vitality. The shamans of ancient Mexico believed that mixing energy in this fashion makes it possible to separate the energy of both bodies more readily by dropping unfamiliar energy into them, a process which they described as *exacerbating the centers of vitality.*

17. Bunching Necessary Energy and Dispersing Unnecessary Energy
This magical pass entails movements that could best be described as

Figure 239   Figure 240

pushing something solid across the front of the body with the palm of the hand, and dragging it back across the front of the body with the back of the hand.

It starts with the left arm kept close to the body, by the waist, with the forearm bent at a ninety-degree angle. The forearm is brought closer to the body as the movement begins, and the hand is bent back at the wrist. The palm of the left hand faces right; the thumb is locked. Then, as if a great force were opposing it, it moves across the body to the extreme right, without the elbow losing its ninety-degree angle (fig. 239). From there, again as if a great force were opposing it, the hand is dragged as far left as it can reach without losing the ninety-degree angle of the elbow, with the palm still facing the right (fig. 240).

During this entire sequence of movements, the muscles of the left body are contracted to the maximum, and the right arm is held immobile against the right leg.

The same sequence of movements is repeated with the right arm and hand.

18. Piling Energy onto the Left and Right Bodies
The weight is placed on the right leg. The knee is slightly bent for support and balance. The left leg and arm, which are kept semitense, sweep in front of the body in an arc from left to right, in unison. The left foot and the left hand end at a position just to the right of the body. The outer edge of the left foot touches the ground. The fingertips of the left hand point down as the sweep is made (fig. 241). Then both the left leg and the left arm return to their original positions.

The exact sequence is repeated by sweeping the right leg and arm to the left.

Figure 241

19. Gathering Energy with One Arm and Striking It with the Other
Don Juan said that with this magical pass, energy was stirred and collected with the movement of one arm and was struck with the movement of the opposite arm. He believed that striking, with one hand, energy which had been gathered by the other, allowed the entrance of

energy into one body from sources belonging to the other body, something which was never done under normal conditions.

The left arm moves up to the level of the eyes. The wrist is slightly bent backwards; in this position, going from left to right and back again, the hand draws the figure of an oval, about a foot and a half wide and as long as the width of the body (fig. 242). Then the hand, with the palm facing down, moves across at eye level from left to right as if cutting through, with the tips of the fingers, the figure which it has drawn (fig. 243).

At the moment that the left hand reaches the level of the right shoulder, the right hand, which is held at waist level with the cupped palm turned upward, shoots forward, striking with the heel of the hand, to hit the spot in the middle of the oval drawn by the left hand, as the left hand is slowly brought down (fig. 244). As it strikes, the palm of the right hand is facing forward, and the fingers are slightly curved, permitting in this fashion the necessary contour of the palm to strike a round surface. The strike ends with the elbow slightly bent, to avoid over-stretching the tendons.

The same movements are performed beginning with the right arm.

Figure 242

Figure 243

Figure 244

20. Gathering Energy with the Arms and Legs
The body pivots slightly to the right on the ball of the right foot; the left leg juts out at a forty-five-degree angle, with the knee bent to give a

forward slant to the trunk. The body is made to rock three times, as if to gain momentum. Then the left arm scoops downward as if to grab something at the level of the left knee (fig. 245). The body leans back, and with that impulse, the lower part of the left leg, from the knee down, is brought close to the groin, almost touching it with the heel; the left hand swiftly brushes the vital area of the liver and gallbladder, on the right (fig. 246).

Figure 245   Figure 246

The same sequence of movements is repeated with the right leg and arm, which bring the gathered energy to the center of vitality located around the pancreas and spleen, on the left.

21. Moving Energy from the Left and the Right Shoulders
The left arm moves from its natural position hanging by the left thigh to the right shoulder, where it grabs something, and the hand turns into a fist. This movement is propelled by a sharp twist of the waist to the right. The knees are slightly bent to allow this turning movement. The acutely bent elbow is not allowed to sag, but is kept at the level of the shoulders (fig. 247). Propelled by a straightening of the waist, the fist is then moved away from the right shoulder in an upward arc, striking, with the back of the hand, a point slightly above the head and in line with the left shoulder (fig. 248). The hand opens there as if to drop something that is held in the fist.

The same sequence of movements is repeated with the right arm.

Figure 247

Figure 248

22. Gathering Energy from One Body and Dispersing It on the Other

Beginning from its natural position by the left thigh, the left arm draws an arc from left to right, crossing in front of the pubis until it reaches the extreme right. This movement is aided by a slight turn of the waist. From there, the arm continues moving in a circle above the head, to the height and level of the left shoulder. It cuts across then to the level of the right shoulder. There, the hand turns into a fist, as if grabbing something, with the palm down (Fig. 249). Next, the fist hits a point at the height of the head, an arm's length away from it. The blow is delivered with the soft edge of the hand, using the hand as if it were a hammer.

Figure 249

Figure 250

The arm is fully extended, but slightly curved at the elbow (fig. 250).

The same movements are repeated with the right arm.

23. Hammering Energy from the Left Shoulder and the Right Shoulder on the Midpoint in Front of the Face

The left arm is moved above the head. The elbow is bent at a ninety-degree angle. The hand turns there into a fist, with the palm facing upward. Then it strikes from the left, with the soft edge of the hand, the division line of the left and right body, in front of the face. The body leans slightly to the left as this strike is made (fig. 251). The fisted hand keeps on moving until it almost touches the right shoulder; the palm turns there so that it faces downward. Then it makes a similar strike, this time from the right; the body leans to the right (fig. 252).

This same sequence of movements is repeated with the right arm.

A reservoir of neutral energy can be built by this magical pass, meaning energy which can easily be used by either the left body or the right body.

Figure 251   Figure 252

24. A Strike with the Hand Fisted at the Second Knuckle

Both arms are lifted to the level of the neck, the elbows held at ninety-degree angles. The hands are held with the fingers bent at the second knuckle and held tightly over the palm (figs. 253, 254). From this position, the left hand strikes. The strike is a powerful swing made to the right, across the line of the right shoulder, but without greatly moving the arm. The arm is driven by a powerful rightward twist of the waist (fig. 255).

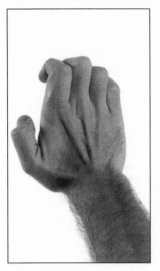

Figure 253 *Figure 254* *Figure 255*

The right arm moves in the same fashion beyond the line of the left shoulder, driven by an instantaneous leftward twist of the waist.

25. Grabbing Energy from the Shoulders and Smashing It on the Centers of Vitality

The left arm moves to the right shoulder, and the hand turns into a fist, as if grabbing something (fig. 256). The elbow is kept bent at a ninety-

Figure 256 *Figure 257* *Figure 258*

degree angle. Then the fist is forcefully brought back to the left side by the waist (fig. 257). It stays there for an instant to gain impulse, and then the fist shoots across the body to the right, the fisted palm facing the body, to strike through a point by the area of the liver and gallbladder (fig. 258).

The same movement is repeated with the right arm, which strikes across the area of the pancreas and spleen.

26. Pushing Energy to the Sides with the Elbows
Both arms are brought to the level of the shoulders, the elbows bent sharply and protruding straight out. The wrists are crossed making a letter X, the left forearm on top of the right one. The hands, clenched into fists, touch the pectoral muscles at the edges of the axillae; the left fist touches the edges of the right axilla and the right fist the edges of the left axilla (fig. 259). The elbows are then forcefully brought out to the sides in line with the shoulders, as if to give an elbow blow to the sides (fig. 260).

This movement is repeated with the right arm on top of the left.

Figure 259   Figure 260

27. Drawing Two Inward Circles of Energy in Front of the Body and Crushing Them Out to the Sides
As a deep breath is taken, the arms circle in unison from their natural position at the sides of the thighs, to the line that separates the left and

the right bodies. This movement ends with the forearms crossed over the chest. The fingers are kept tightly together, pointing upward, the thumbs locked; the wrists are bent at ninety-degree angles. The left arm is on top of the right one. The locked thumb of the left hand touches the pectoral muscle of the right body, and the locked thumb of the right hand touches the pectoral muscle of the left body (fig. 261). The inhalation ends there. A quick exhalation is made as the arms are spread apart forcefully with the hands clenched into fists, each striking, with the back of the hand, a point on the respective sides above the head (fig. 262).

The same movements are repeated with the right arm on top of the left.

Figure 261   *Figure 262*

28. Striking Energy in Front of the Body and on the Left and Right with Both Fists

The hands are clenched into fists at the level of the waist. The palms of the fists face each other. Both hands are lifted to the level of the eyes and strike forcefully downward in unison at two points in front of the groin; they hit the target with the soft part of the fists (fig. 263). From there, the arms swing in unison, making an upward arc to the left as the whole trunk leans toward the left, following the impulse of the arms. The fists strike with the knuckles (fig. 264). The fists return to deliver another blow to the same points in front of the groin. From there, the arms swing in unison, making an upward arc to the right as the whole trunk leans toward the right, following the impulse of the arms. The fists strike with the knuckles. The fists move one more time to deliver a blow with the soft edge of the hands to the same two points in front of the groin.

Figure 263   Figure 264

29. Striking Energy in Front of the Body with Both Fists and on the Left and the Right

The beginning of this magical pass is exactly like the preceding one (fig. 265). Once the strike is completed, both arms are lifted like hammers to the level of the head, and the trunk is made to turn sharply to the left. The two fists strike two points in front of the left hip (fig. 266). The

Figure 265   Figure 266   Figure 267

arms lift again to the height of the head, the palms of the hands are opened, and they descend to strike the same two points (fig. 267). The arms are raised again to the level of the head. The hands turn into fists to strike the same points once again. The forearms are raised to the level of the head, the body turns to face the front, and the fists are slammed down on the same points in front of the groin.

The same sequence of movements is repeated with the trunk turned sharply to the right.

30. Smashing Energy with the Wrists Above the Head and on the Left and the Right

Both hands are raised above the head, with the wrists touching and the palms curved as if holding a ball (fig. 268). Then the trunk turns to the left, as both arms move sharply to the left of the waist without disengaging the wrists, which rotate on each other to accommodate the new position of the hands. The palm of the left hand faces upward, and the palm of the right hand faces downward (fig. 269). Both arms are moved to the point above the head again, still without disengaging the wrists, which rotate to adopt their initial position.

The same sequence of movements is performed by bringing the hands sharply to a point to the right of the waist. The movement ends by bringing the hands back to their starting position above the head.

Figure 268

Figure 269

The Third Group:
Moving the Energy of the Left Body and the Right Body with the Breath

The third group consists of nine magical passes that employ inhalations and exhalations as their driving force to either further separate or join the two bodies. As already stated, in the view of the sorcerers of don Juan's lineage, putting a dab of energy from one body into any vital center of the other creates a much sought-for momentary agitation in that center. The sorcerers of ancient Mexico, according to what don Juan taught, considered this mixing to be extremely beneficial because it breaks the fixed, routine input of those centers. Those sorcerers felt that breathing is a key issue in the separation of the left body and the right body.

31. The Breath for the Upper Fringe of the Lungs

The arms, with the hands clenched into fists, are raised to the forehead with a deep inhalation; the palms of the fisted hands face down. The fists are three or four inches from each other, right in front of the forehead, as the inhalation ends (fig. 270). An exhalation is made as the arms spread forcefully to two lateral points to the sides and even with the shoulders (fig. 271). The hands relax and open. The wrists cross in front of the head and a deep inhalation is taken as the arms make two

Figure 270   Figure 271   Figure 272   Figure 273

big circles the length of the arms, going from the front, up over the head, and to the sides. The inhalation ends as the hands come to rest by the waist, with the palms up (fig. 272). A slow exhalation is made then, while the hands are raised along the edges of the rib cage, to the level of the axillae. The exhalation ends as the shoulders are pushed up, as if the force of the hands were making them rise (fig. 273).

This breath is a true bonus because it allows the mobilization of the upper part of the lungs, a thing which hardly ever happens under normal conditions.

32. Offering the Breath

The left arm draws a circle as a deep inhalation is taken. It moves from the front to above the head, to the back, to the front again; as the arm rotates, the trunk turns to the left, to allow the arm to move in a full circle. The inhalation ends when the circle is completed. The palm of the hand is held at the level of the chin; it faces up, and the wrist is bent at a ninety-degree angle. The posture of the practitioner is that of one who is offering something which is placed on the palm. The trunk is bent forward (fig. 274). The palm of the hand is then turned to face down, and an exhalation begins while the arm moves slowly and powerfully downward (fig. 275) to rest on the left side by the thigh; the palm is still facing down, and the back of the hand maintains the ninety-degree angle in relation to the forearm.

The same sequence of movements is executed with the right arm.

Figure 274

Figure 275

33. Moving Energy with the Breath from the Top of the Head to the Vital Centers

The wrists of both arms are slightly bent; the palms of the hands are semicurled. With the hands in this position, the tips of the fingers brush upward along the front of the body and over the head as a deep inhalation is made (fig. 276). When the arms reach their full extension above the head, the hands are straightened and the wrists are turned back at a ninety-degree angle. The inhalation ends there. While the hands are brought down, the air is held, and the index finger of each hand is raised; the other fingers are held against the palm, bent at the second knuckle, and the thumbs are locked. Both arms are retrieved to the level of the chest, with the back of the hands against the axillae.

A deep exhalation begins then as the arms are slowly extended straight forward until the elbows are gently locked. A deep inhalation then is taken as the hands are retrieved back to the position against the axillae, still with the index fingers raised, the wrists bent backwards, the palms facing forward. A slow exhalation begins while the hands move upward in a circle that first reaches above the head and then continues downward, making a complete forward circle without changing the position of the index fingers. The hands come to rest by the sides of the rib cage (fig. 277). The exhalation ends as the hands are pushed downward to the sides of the hips.

Figure 276

Figure 277

34. Shattering Energy with the Breath

As a deep inhalation is taken, the left hand moves in a wide side circle from the front, to above the head, to the back. The trunk turns to the left to facilitate the full rotation of the arm. The inhalation ends when the arm has made a full turn and stops at a place to the side of the head and above it. The palm of the hand faces forward; the wrist is slightly turned back (fig. 278). A slow exhalation begins then as the arm makes another wide side circle in the opposite direction, going from the front down to the back, then above the head, and to the front again. When the circle is completed, the arm is brought to a point just in front of the right shoulder as the exhalation continues. The palm is facing the body and lightly touches the right shoulder (fig. 279). Then the arm shoots out laterally with the hand clenched in a fist and strikes, with the back of the hand, a point an arm's length away from the left shoulder at the height of the head (fig. 280). The exhalation ends there.

The same sequence of movements is repeated with the right arm.

Figure 278   Figure 279   Figure 280

35. The Monkey Breath

The knees are slightly bent. The arms are lifted slowly over the head as the upper part of the lungs is filled with air. Then the knees become locked and the body is fully extended upward. This breath can be taken either with the heels on the ground, or on the tips of the toes.

The breath is held as the arms move downward and the body stoops slightly forward, contracting the diaphragm; the knees are bent again. The exhalation begins when the hands reach the level of the waist. At the same time, the index fingers are extended and point to the ground; the other fingers are contracted over the palms of the hands. The hands continue moving downward as all the air is exhaled (fig. 281). While exhaling, the diaphragm is held tight in order to avoid pushing it downward with the exhaling air.

Figure 281

36. The Altitude Breath

The legs are held as straight as possible. An inhalation begins while the shoulders slowly rotate from the front to the back with the arms bent at the elbows. When the rotation and the inhalation end, the arms are kept in the initial position (fig. 282). The exhalation begins by raising the hands to the level of the shoulders and extending the arms as far forward as possible with the palms facing the ground.

Next, an inhalation is taken as the palms of the hands are turned upward. The elbows are bent and pulled all the way back, and the shoulders are raised. The inhalation ends with the maximum upward stretch of the shoulders (fig. 283).

An exhalation is made as the palms are turned to face the ground and

Figure 282   *Figure 283*

the hands and shoulders push downward; the hands are bent backward at the wrists as far as possible, and the arms are held straight at the sides of the body.

37. The Lateral Breath

As an inhalation begins, the arms move from their natural position by the sides of the thighs in a circle toward the center of the body, ending with the arms crossed; the palms face outward, and the wrists are fully bent so that the fingertips point upward (fig. 284). The inhalation continues while the two arms are pushed out laterally. As the arms move, the palms of the hands first face forward; when the movement ends, they face away from each other. The inhalation ends at the maximum extension of the arms. The body is kept as erect as possible (fig. 285).

An exhalation is made by bending the arms at the elbows as the palms of the hands, with the fingertips raised upward, come toward the center of the body, pass it, and cross to end at the opposite edges of the body. The left forearm is on top of the right. The body is contracted at the midsection, and the knees are bent (fig. 286).

Figure 284   Figure 285   Figure 286

38. The Butterfly Breath

The arms are bent at the elbows and held in front of the chest. The left forearm is held above the right one without touching it; the wrists are straight and the hands are clenched into fists. The knees are bent, and the body stoops forward markedly (fig. 287). As an inhalation begins, the arms separate and move up over the head and out to the left and right. As the inhalation continues, the arms straighten as they circle, going down, to the sides, and around the shoulders, and then fold back to their initial position over the chest. Maintaining their position, the arms are raised over the head, as the breath is held and the body straightens at the waist (fig. 288). Then the arms are brought down to the level of the umbilical region as the body goes back into the initial stooped-forward position, with bent knees.

The body holds that stooped-forward position steadily, and an exhalation is made by repeating the same movements of the arms done for the inhalation. As the air is expelled, the diaphragm is kept in a tight position.

Figure 287   Figure 288

39. Breathing Out Through the Elbows

At the beginning of this movement, the legs are kept straight. As a deep breath is taken, the arms make outward circles above the head and around the sides of the body. The inhalation ends with the arms pointing straight out to the front, elbows bent, at the level of the waist. The palms are held straight and facing each other; the fingers are together.

An exhalation begins as the hands point to the ground at a forty-five-degree angle. The knees are bent and the body leans forward (fig. 289). The exhalation continues while the arms, bent at the elbows in a ninety-degree angle, are raised over the head. The body straightens and leans backward slightly. This is achieved by bending the knees, rather than arching the back. The exhalation ends with the abdominal muscles tensed to the maximum; the head is tilted slightly backward (fig. 290).

Practicing this breath creates the sensation that air is being expelled through the elbows.

Figure 289

Figure 290

The Fourth Group:
The Predilection of the Left Body and the Right Body

This group is composed of five magical passes for the left body executed in a sequence, and three magical passes for the right body. According to don Juan Matus, the predilection of the left body is silence, while the predilection of the right body is chatter, noise, sequential order. He said that it is the right body which forces us to march, because it likes parades, and it's most delighted with choreography, sequences, and arrangements that entail classification by size.

Don Juan recommended that the performance of each movement of the magical passes for the right be repeated many times, as the practitioners count, and that it is very important to set up beforehand the number of times in which any given movement is going to be repeated, because prediction is the forte of the right body. If the practitioners set up any number beforehand and fulfill it, the pleasure of the right body is indescribable.

In the practice of Tensegrity, however, both the magical passes for the left body and the magical passes for the right body are performed in complete silence. If the silence of the left body can be made to overlap onto the right body, the act of *saturation* can become a direct way to enter what don Juan called the most coveted state that the shamans of every generation sought: *inner silence*.

THE FIVE MAGICAL PASSES FOR THE LEFT BODY

The magical passes for the left body have no individual names. Don Juan said that the shamans of ancient Mexico called them just *magical passes for the left body*.

The first magical pass consists of fifteen carefully executed brief movements. Since the magical passes for the left body are done in a sequence, they are going to be numbered sequentially.

1. The left arm moves laterally about a foot away from its natural position by the thigh (fig. 291).

2. The palm is turned sharply to face the front as the elbow is slightly bent (fig. 292).

3. The hand is raised to the level of the navel and cuts across to the right (fig. 293).

Figure 291   *Figure 292*   *Figure 293*

4. The hand is turned sharply until the palm faces down (fig. 294).

5. The hand cuts across from right to left with the palm of the hand facing down (fig. 295).

6. The wrist turns sharply to the right; the hand is cupped, as if to scoop something, and the movement of the wrist makes it move upward with a jolt (fig. 296).

Figure 294

Figure 295

Figure 296

7. The arm is raised in an arc in front of the line dividing the two bodies to the level of the eyes, a foot away from it, with the palm of the hand facing left (fig. 297).

Figure 297

Figure 298

Figure 299

8. The wrist turns, making the hand face forward (fig. 298).

9. The arm goes out over the head, draws a lateral circle, and returns to the same position in front of the eyes with the palm of the hand facing left (fig. 299).

10. The wrist moves again to make the palm of the hand face forward (fig. 300).

Figure 300

Figure 301

Figure 302

11. The hand moves down toward the left, in a slight curve to the level of the shoulders, with the palm facing the ground (fig. 301).

12. The wrist is turned so the palm faces up (fig. 302).

Figure 303

Figure 304

Figure 305

13. The hand cuts to the right, to a point in front of the right shoulder (fig. 303).

14. The wrist moves again, turning the palm down (fig. 304).

15. The hand sweeps down to a position about a foot in front of the left hip (fig. 305).

The second magical pass is composed of nine movements.

16. The hand is retrieved and touches the crest of the hip (fig. 306).

17. The elbow moves out laterally, and the wrist, by a sharp downward movement, turns the palm to face the left. The palm of the hand is cupped, the fingers slightly spread (fig. 307).

18. The arm makes a full circle, going over the head from front to back. The hand returns to the crest of the hip with the palm facing up (fig. 308).

Figure 306

Figure 307

Figure 308

19. The elbow moves out laterally again, and another quick movement of the wrist turns the palm to face the left again (fig. 309).

20. The hand moves to the side to make a circle as if scooping something. At the end of the movement, the hand returns to a position at the crest of the hip with the palm facing up (fig. 310).

21. The bent elbow moves sharply to the left at the same time that a quick turn of the wrist turns the hand back; the fingers, slightly curved, point to the back; the palm is hollowed and faces up (fig. 311).

22. Then the elbow is fully extended to the back while the palm of the cupped hand still faces up (fig. 312).

Figure 309   Figure 310   Figure 311

23. While the arm is still fully extended, the wrist turns over slowly, making a full rotation, until the palm faces up again (fig. 313).

24. This movement resembles pulling the arm out of a sleeve. Leading with the elbow, the arm draws a circle from back to front, and the movement ends with the palm of the hand up, at the level of the edge of the rib cage, and the bent elbow touching the edge of the ribs (fig. 314).

Figure 312   Figure 313   Figure 314

The third magical pass is made up of twelve movements.

25. The hand moves in an arc to the right with the palm facing up, as

if cutting something with the tips of the fingers, stopping a foot past the right edge of the rib cage (fig. 315).

26. The palm of the hand is turned to face the ground (fig. 316).

27. The arm moves in an arc to the left and then all the way to the back (fig. 317).

28. The palm of the hand is hollow, the arm is fully extended, and the turn of the wrist makes the hand into a scoop (fig. 318).

Figure 315

Figure 316

Figure 317

29. The hand moves above the head, following a diagonal course from the back to the front that ends above the right shoulder at the level of the head (fig. 319).

Figure 318

Figure 319

Figure 320

30. The hand is straightened out and the wrist is contracted to place it in a ninety-degree angle with the forearm. The hand descends this way from above the head to the right of the waist (fig. 320).

31. The palm is turned briskly downward (fig. 321).

32. The arm swings in a half-circle all the way to the left and to the back (fig. 322).

Figure 321

Figure 322

Figure 323

33. The palm turns up (fig. 323).

34. The arm swings to the front, to the same position on the right, a foot away from the rib cage (fig. 324).

35. The hand is turned so the palm faces the ground again (fig. 325).

Figure 324

Figure 325

Figure 326

36. The arm swings to the left and returns to the same point behind the back on the left side (fig. 326).

The fourth magical pass consists of fifteen movements.

37. The arm swings in a big circle to the front, above the head, and to the back, and ends at a point about a foot away from the left thigh (fig. 327).

Figure 327   Figure 328   Figure 329

38. The head is turned to the left. The elbow is bent sharply and the forearm is raised to the level of the eyes, with the palm of the hand facing outward, as if shielding the eyes from light glare. The body stoops forward (fig. 328).

Figure 330   Figure 331   Figure 332

39. The head and trunk rotate slowly all the way to the right, as if to look in the distance with a shield over the eyes (fig. 329).

40. The head and trunk rotate again to the left (fig. 330).

41. The palm of the hand is quickly turned to face up as the head and trunk move to look straight forward (fig. 331).

42. Then the hand cuts a line in front of the body from left to right (fig. 332).

43. The palm is turned to face down (fig. 333).

44. The arm sweeps to the left (fig. 334).

45. The wrist is turned again in order to have the palm facing up (fig. 335).

| Figure 333 | Figure 334 | Figure 335 |

46. The arm cuts another arc in front of the body to the right (fig. 336).

47. The position of the hand is changed again; the palm faces down (fig. 337).

48. The arm sweeps again to the left (fig. 338).

49. The palm is turned to face upward (fig. 339).

50. The arm makes a line across the front of the body to the right (fig. 340).

51. The palm is turned to face down (fig. 341).

Figure 336

Figure 337

Figure 338

Figure 339

Figure 340

Figure 341

The fifth magical pass is made up of twenty-five movements.

52. The hand draws a large circle in front of the body, with the palm of the hand facing forward as the circle is drawn. The movement ends at a point in front of the right shoulder; the palm is facing up (fig. 342).

53. The elbow turns up as the wrist and hand turn to face down. The palm of the hand is slightly hollowed (fig. 343).

54. The hand draws an oval-shaped line from right to left as if scooping a chunk of matter. When it comes to the position where it started, the palm is facing up (fig. 344).

55. The hand drops to the level of the groin, fingers pointing to the ground (fig. 345).

Figure 342

Figure 343

Figure 344

Figure 345

Figure 346

Figure 347

56. The palm of the hand is turned to face the body (fig. 346).

57. Then it moves, following the contour of the body, fingers pointing toward the ground, to a place four or five inches away from the left thigh (fig. 347).

58. A quick turn of the wrist makes the palm face the thigh (fig. 348).

59. The head turns to the left as the hand is raised, as if rubbing the fingers along a straight surface, to the level of the eyes (fig. 349).

60. From there, it descends at an angle to a point slightly to the left side of the groin. The head follows the movement of the hand (fig. 350).

61. The hand is raised again to the level of the eyes, at an angle. It

Figure 348

Figure 349

Figure 350

reaches a point exactly on the division line of the left and right bodies, right in front of the eyes, a foot and a half away from them (fig. 351).

62. The hand descends again at an angle, to a point in front and slightly to the right of the groin (fig. 352).

63. The hand is raised again, drawing another slanted line, to a point in front of the eyes in line with the shoulders; the head follows the movement to the right (fig. 353).

64. The hand descends in a straight line to a point a foot away from the right thigh (fig. 354).

In the seven preceding movements, three peaks have been drawn, the

Figure 351

Figure 352

Figure 353

first one on the left, the second one on the very center dividing line, and the third to the right.

65. The hand changes position so the palm faces left (fig. 355).

66. The hand is raised to draw a curved line that fits exactly in between the right and center peaks drawn before (fig. 356).

Figure 354

Figure 355

Figure 356

67. There the palm of the hand is made to face the right (fig. 357).

68. The hand descends to the level of the groin and stops at the dividing line between the left and the right bodies (fig. 358).

69. The palm changes directions there again and faces left (fig. 359).

Figure 357

Figure 358

Figure 359

Figure 360   Figure 361   Figure 362

70. The hand is raised to a point between the middle peak and the left peak at the level of the eyes (fig. 360).

71. The palm is turned to face right (fig. 361).

72. The hand descends all the way down to the point in front of the thigh where it began (fig. 362).

The peaks drawn in the eight movements of this second phase are slightly round, as opposed to the very angular peaks drawn before.

73. The hand is turned once more to have the palm face forward (fig. 363).

74. The arm moves over the head as if to pour on the right face and body an invisible substance (fig. 364).

Figure 363   Figure 364

75. The hand is dropped down (fig. 365). Making a half-circle, the elbow rotates to the back (fig. 366).

76. As if it were a knife going into its sheath, the hand slides over the center of vitality around the pancreas and the spleen (fig. 367).

Figure 365   Figure 366   Figure 367

THE THREE MAGICAL PASSES FOR THE RIGHT BODY

The first magical pass for the right body consists of five movements.

1. The right hand, at a ninety-degree angle to the forearm and with the palm facing front, makes a complete circle from left to right, to the level of the right ear, and comes to rest at the same position that it started, about a foot in front of the waist (fig. 368).

2. From there, the arm moves in a sharp arc at the level of the chest by acutely bending the elbow. The palm faces the ground; the fingers are held together and straight with the thumb locked. The index finger and thumb nearly touch the chest (fig. 369).

3. The forearm moves briskly away from the chest so that the elbow is bent at a forty-five-degree angle (fig. 370).

4. The hand rotates on the wrist; the fingers point to the ground for an instant and then flip up above the head, as if the hand were a knife (fig. 371).

5. The hand descends. Using its outer edge as if it were a cutting tool, it cuts to the level of the navel (fig. 372).

Figure 368   Figure 369   Figure 370

Figure 371   Figure 372

The second magical pass for the right body consists of the following twelve movements.

6. From the side of the waist, the hand shoots out to a point in front of the body. At the arm's maximum extension, the fingers separate (figs. 373, 374).

7. The arm is retrieved to the level of the waist. The elbow protrudes back, sharply bent (fig. 375).

8. The hand is turned so that the palm faces up (fig. 376).

9. The arm is extended forward with the palm open and facing up (fig. 377).

Figure 373

Figure 374

Figure 375

Figure 376

Figure 377

Figure 378

10. With the palm still facing up, the arm returns again to the level of the waist (fig. 378).

11. The palm is turned to face downward (fig. 379).

12. The arm makes a full side circle, going to the back, above the head, and to the front, and ends in front of the navel by slamming the palm down as if it were hitting something solid (fig. 380).

13. The palm is turned toward the body, in a movement that resembles the action of gathering something on the right body (fig. 381).

14. The arm is raised above the head as if the hand were a knife that is being wielded (fig. 382).

Figure 379

Figure 380

Figure 381

Figure 382

Figure 383

Figure 384

Figure 385

15. It makes a diagonal cut to the midpoint in front of the body, a foot and a half away from it. The palm is facing left (fig. 383).

16. The hand, with the palm straight, is raised to the level of the face, in a straight line (fig. 384).

17. It makes a diagonal cut with the palm slightly slanted downward to a point in front of the edge of the right body, a foot and a half away from it (fig. 385).

The third magical pass for the right body is made up of twelve movements.

18. The right arm, with the elbow sharply bent toward the right and the hand held with the palm toward the body, moves in an arc from the right side to a point in front of the solar plexus (fig. 386).

19. Pivoting on the elbow, the forearm makes a quarter of a circle downward, turning the palm to face the right side (fig. 387).

20. The arm makes a small outward circle, from left to right, going up, then down again, and ending with the palm by the waist, facing up (figs. 388a, 388b).

Figure 386   Figure 387   Figure 388a   Figure 388b

21. Another circle from the front to the back is made. It ends up at the point where it started, with the palm of the hand facing up (fig. 389).

22. The palm is turned to face down (fig. 390).

23. The hand then moves slowly to the front (fig. 391).

24. The wrist is turned so the palm faces the left. With a straight palm, fingers held tightly together, and thumb locked, the hand is raised straight up as if it were a knife (fig. 392).

25. Then it draws a small convex arc to the left, so that the palm flips to face right, and cuts straight down just to the left of the line drawn previously, to the level of the navel (fig. 393).

26. With the hand still facing right, it moves upward and retraces the same line it drew before (fig. 394).

In the preceding three movements, a long oval figure has been drawn.

27. Then the hand cuts down, as if to cut off one-third of the long figure (fig. 395).

Figure 389

Figure 390

Figure 391

Figure 392

Figure 393

Figure 394

Figure 395

28. The palm turns to face right again (fig. 396).

29. It scoops whatever it has cut and has turned into a ball, and splashes it on the front of the right body (figs. 397, 398).

30. The hand is dropped down to the crest of the right hip (fig. 399).

31. The hand rotates as the arm makes a half-circle going from the front (fig. 400) to the back, stopping behind the right shoulder (fig. 401).

32. As if it were a knife going into its sheath, the hand slides over the energy center around the liver and gallbladder (figs. 402, 403).

Figure 396

Figure 397

Figure 398

Figure 399

Figure 400

Figure 401

Figure 402

Figure 403

The Masculinity Series

Masculinity was the name given to a specific group of magical passes by the shamans who first discovered and used them. Don Juan thought that perhaps it was the oldest name given to any such group of magical passes. This group was practiced originally for generations only by male shaman practitioners, and this discrimination in favor of male shamans was done not out of necessity, but rather for reasons of ritual and to satisfy an original drive for male supremacy. Nevertheless, this drive was soon terminated under the impact of enhanced perception.

The well-established tradition of this group of magical passes being practiced only by men persisted in a pseudo-official way for generations while it was being practiced on the sly by female practitioners as well. The old sorcerers' rationale for including females was that for reasons of strife and social disorder around them, the women needed extra strength and vitality, which they believed was found only in males who practiced this group of magical passes. Therefore, women were allowed to execute the movements as a token of solidarity. In don Juan's time, the division lines between males and females became even more diffused. The secrecy and exclusivity of the old sorcerers was completely shattered, and even the old rationale for allowing women to practice these specific magical passes could not be upheld. Female practitioners performed these magical passes openly.

The value of this group of magical passes—the oldest named group in existence—is its continuity. All of its magical passes were generic from the beginning, and this condition provided the only instance in don Juan's lineage of sorcerers in which a whole party of shaman practitioners, whatever their number may have been, were allowed to move in unison. The number of participants in any party of sorcerers, throughout the ages, could never have been more than sixteen. Therefore, none of those sorcerers were ever in the position to witness the stupendous energetic contribution of human mass. For them, there existed only the specialized consensus of a few initiates, a consensus which brought in the possibility of idiosyncratic preferences and more isolationism.

The fact that the movements of Tensegrity are practiced in seminars and workshops by hundreds of participants at the same time has given rise, as stated before, to the possibility of experiencing the energetic effects of human mass. Such an energetic effect is twofold: not only are the participants of Tensegrity performing an activity that unites them energetically, but they are also involved in a quest delineated in states of enhanced awareness by the shamans of ancient Mexico: the *redeployment of energy*. Performing these magical passes in the setting of seminars on Tensegrity is a unique experience. It permits the participants to arrive, pushed or pulled by the magical passes themselves and by the human mass, at energetic conclusions never even alluded to in don Juan's teachings.

The reason for calling this set of movements *Masculinity* is its aggressive quality, and because its magical passes are very brisk and forcefully executed, characteristics easily identified with maleness. Don Juan stated that their practice fostered not only a sensation of well-being, but a *special sensorial quality*, which, if not examined, could easily be confused with strife and aggressiveness. However, if it is carefully scrutinized, it is immediately apparent that it is, rather, an unmistakable sensation of readiness that places the practitioners at a level from which they could strike toward the unknown.

Another reason that the shamans of ancient Mexico called this group of magical passes *Masculinity* was because the males who practiced it became a special type of practitioner who didn't need to be taken by the hand. They became men who benefited indirectly from everything they did. Ideally, the energy generated by this group of magical passes goes to the centers of vitality themselves, as if every center made an automatic bidding for energy, which goes first to the center that needs it the most.

For don Juan Matus's disciples, this set of magical passes became the most crucial element in their training. Don Juan himself introduced it to them as a common denominator, meaning that he urged them to practice the set unaltered. What he wanted was to prepare his disciples to withstand the rigors of journeying in the unknown.

In Tensegrity, the word *Series* has been added to the name *Masculinity* to put it on a par with the other series of Tensegrity. The Masculinity Series is divided into three groups, each consisting of ten magical passes. The goal of the first and second groups of the Masculinity Series is the tuning of *tendon energy*. Each of these twenty magical passes is short, but extremely focused. Tensegrity practitioners are seriously encouraged, as the shamanistic practitioners of ancient times were, to get the maximum effect from the short movements by aiming to release a jolt of *tendon energy* every time they execute them.

"But don't you think, don Juan, that every time I release this jolt of energy, I'm actually wasting my *tendon energy*, and draining it out of me?" I asked him on one occasion.

"You can't drain any energy out of yourself," he said. "The energy that you are seemingly wasting by delivering a jolt to the air is not really being wasted, because it never leaves your boundaries, wherever those boundaries may be. So what you're really doing is delivering a jolt of energy to what the sorcerers of ancient Mexico called our 'crust,' our 'bark.' Those sorcerers stated that energetically, human beings are like *luminous balls* that have a thick peel around them, like an orange; some of them have something even harder and thicker, like the bark of an old tree."

Don Juan explained carefully that this simile of human beings being like an orange was somehow misleading because the peel or the bark that we have is located inside our boundaries, just as if an orange had its peel inside the orange itself. He said that this bark or peel was the crusted-down energy that had been discarded throughout our lifetime from our vital centers of energy, because of the wear and tear of daily life.

"Is it beneficial to hit this bark, don Juan?" I asked.

"Most beneficial," he said. "Especially if the practitioners aim all their *intent* at reaching that bark with their blows. If they *intend* to shatter portions of this crusted-down energy by means of the magical passes, that shattered energy could be absorbed by the vital centers of energy."

The magical passes of the third group of the Masculinity Series are broader, more extensive. What practitioners need in order to execute the ten magical passes of the third group is steadiness of the hands, the legs, and the rest of the body. The aim of this third series, for the shamans of ancient Mexico, was the building of endurance, of stability.

Those shamans believed that holding the body steadily in position while executing those long movements gives the practitioners a foothold from which they can stand on their own.

What modern practitioners of Tensegrity have found out through their practice is that the Masculinity Series can be executed only in moderation, in order to avoid overtiring the tendons of the arms and the muscles of the back.

The First Group:
Magical Passes in Which the Hands
Are Moved in Unison but Held Separately

1. Fists Above the Shoulders

The hands are held by the sides, clasped into fists, the palms facing up. They are raised then to a point above the head by bending the elbows so the forearms are at a ninety-degree angle with the upper arms. The driving force of this movement is equally divided between the muscles of the arms and the contraction of the muscles of the abdomen. As the fists are

Figure 404

Figure 405

raised and the muscles of the front of the body are tensed, the body leans slightly backward by bending the knees (fig. 404). The arms, with hands fisted, are brought down to the sides of the thighs by straightening the elbows a bit; as the arms move down, the body leans forward, contracting the muscles of the back and the diaphragm (fig. 405).

2. Using a Cutting Tool in Each Hand

The hands are made into fists, with the palms facing each other at the level of the waist (fig. 406). From there, they move in a downward strike to the level of the groin, a foot and a half away from it, always keeping the width of the body as the distance between the fists (fig. 407). Once the fists strike, they are retrieved to the position where they started, by the edge of the rib cage.

Figure 406

Figure 407

3. Polishing a High Table with the Palms of the Hands

The arms are raised to the level of the axillae. The palms of the hands face down. The elbows, acutely bent, protrude sharply behind the back (fig. 408). Both arms are brought briskly forward to the maximum extension, as if the palms were actually polishing a hard surface. The hands are kept at a distance which equals the width of the body (fig. 409). From there, they are retrieved with equal force to the position where the movement began (fig. 408).

Figure 408

Figure 409

4. Tapping Energy with Both Hands

Both arms are raised to the front, at the level of the shoulders. The hands are held in angular fists, meaning that the position of the fingers slants down heavily as they are held against the palm of the hands. The thumbs are held on top of the outer edge of the index fingers (fig. 410). The palms of the hands face each other. A sharp jolt of the wrists makes the fists go down slightly, but with great force. The level of the wrists never changes; in other words, only the hand pivots down on the wrists.

Figure 410

Figure 411

The counter movement is to raise the fists with a jolt without changing the position of the wrists (fig. 411).

This magical pass is, for shamans, one of the best sources for exercising the *tendon energy* of the arms, because of the number of energy points that exist around the wrists, the backs of the hands, the palms, and the fingers.

Figure 412

5. Jolting Energy

This magical pass is the companion to the preceding one. It begins by raising both arms to the front at the level of the shoulders. The hands are held in angular fists, just as in the preceding magical pass, except that in this one, the palms of the hands are turned to face downward. The fists are moved in toward the body by a jolt of the wrists. Its counterbalancing movement is another jolt of the wrists that sends the fists outward so that the thumbs make a straight line with the rest of the forearm (fig. 412). In order to execute this magical pass, it is required that the muscles of the abdomen are intensely used. It is the action of those muscles which actually directs the jolting of the wrists.

Figure 413

Figure 414

6. Pulling a Rope of Energy

The hands are held in front of the body, at the line that separates the left and the right bodies, as if they were holding a thick rope that hangs from above; the left hand is on top of the right (fig. 413). The magical pass consists in jolting both wrists and making the hands jerk down in a short, powerful movement. As this movement is executed, the muscles of the abdomen contract, and the arms drop down slightly by bending the knees (fig. 414).

Its counterbalancing movement is a jerk of the wrists that jolts the hands upward as the knees and the trunk straighten up a bit (fig. 413).

7. Pushing Down a Pole of Energy

The hands are held to the left of the body, the left hand at the level of the ear, eight or nine inches above the right hand, which is held at the shoulder. They are held as if they were grabbing a thick pole. The palm of the left hand faces the right; and the palm of the right hand faces left. The left hand is the leading hand, by virtue of being on top, and guides the movement (fig. 415). The muscles of the back by the area of the adrenals and the muscles of the abdomen contract, and a powerful push sends both arms downward to the side of the right thigh and the waist, as if they were indeed holding on to a pole (fig. 416). The hands change position there; the right hand moves to a place by the right ear and becomes the leading hand, and the left moves below, by the shoulder, as if the hands were changing poles. The same movements are repeated.

Figure 415

Figure 416

8. Cutting Energy with One Hand at a Time

The fists are raised on the sides until they touch the edge of the rib cage; the palms of the fists face each other (fig. 417). The left arm moves

Figure 417

Figure 418

down in a diagonal line to a point two feet away from the thigh (fig. 418); then it is retrieved (fig. 417). The right arm immediately performs the same movements.

9. Using a Plane of Energy

The left hand is raised to the level of the navel and made into a fist; the elbow is bent at a ninety-degree angle and is held close to the rib cage (fig. 419). The right palm moves as if to slam on top of the left fist. The

Figure 419

Figure 420

Figure 421

Figure 422

right hand stops an inch away from the left (fig. 420). Then it moves four or five inches in front of the fist, in a sharp, cutting movement, as if cutting with the edge of the hand (fig. 421). The left arm is retrieved all the way back by making the elbow protrude backward as far as it can, while the right hand is also retrieved, following the left hand and keeping the same distance (fig. 422). Then, maintaining the same distance between the hands, both the left and the right arm shoot forward to a point a foot and a half or two feet away from the waist.

The same movements are repeated with the fist of the right arm.

10. Striking Energy with a Spike of Energy

The left arm is raised to the level of the shoulders with the elbow bent at a ninety-degree angle. The hand is held as if it had the hilt of a dagger in its grip; the palm faces down. The elbow strikes backward in an arc to a point at the height of the left shoulder, at a forty-five-degree angle behind it (fig. 423). Then the arm returns with a strike along the same arc to its initial position.

The same movement is repeated with the other arm.

Figure 423

The Second Group:
The Magical Passes for Focusing *Tendon Energy*

Figure 424

11. Clasping Hands

Both forearms are brought forward in front of the navel. The bent elbows almost touch the rib cage. The hands are made to clasp, the left hand on top. The fingers of each hand grab the other hand forcefully (fig. 424). All the muscles of the arms and the back are contracted. Then the tense muscles are relaxed and the hands change positions so that the right hand is on top of the left, without letting go of each other, using the hard part of the palm at the base of the fingers as a pivoting surface; the muscles of the arms and back are contracted again.

The same movements are repeated, beginning with the right hand on top.

12. Left and Right Body Clasp

The forearms are brought in front of the body, again at the level of the navel. This time, however, the right forearm is held extended out in a straight line with the hip. It is held close to the rib cage while the left forearm, with the elbow away from the body, puts the left hand over the right one in a clasping position. Great pressure is applied to the palms and the fingers of each hand by the tension of the muscles of the arms, the back, and the abdomen. The tension is relaxed, and the hands are made to pivot on each other's palms, as they move across the body from right to left. There, they are forcefully clasped again, using the same muscles, this time with the right hand on top (fig. 425).

The same movements are repeated from this position.

Figure 425

13. The Sharp Turn of the Two Bodies

The hands are clasped at the level of the waist, to the right. The left hand is on top of the right. In this magical pass, the squeeze of the hands is not as pronounced as the one in the two preceding ones, because what is sought is a sharp turn of the two bodies, rather than the sharp strikes of the two preceding passes.

The clasped hands are made to draw a small circle to the right that goes from the front to the back, and ends in the same position where it started. Since the leading hand is the left hand, by the fact that it is on top, the circle is drawn following the impulse of the left arm, which pushes the hands out first to the right, and around in a circle to the right of the body (fig. 426).

Then the clasped hands move across the front of the body to the left side. Another circle is drawn there, again following the impulse of the left hand.

Figure 426

Being on top, it pulls the other hand to make a circle that goes to the back first, out to the left, and back to the place where it started (fig. 427).

The same sequence of movements is performed with the right hand in the lead, starting at the left by the waist. This time, the impulse of the right arm is followed in order to draw the circle, which goes to the left first, and then back to the same place where it started (fig. 428). The clasped hands move across the front of the body to the right side by the waist. There, following the impulse of the leading hand, they are

Figure 427

Figure 428

Figure 429

pulled back, then to the right, and back where they started, making a circle (fig. 429). It is important that as the circles are drawn, the trunk of the body is turned sharply to the side. The legs remain in the same position, without compensating for the turn by letting the knees sag.

14. Pushing Clasped Energy with the Elbow and Forearm

The hands are clasped by the right side at the level of the shoulder. The upper part of the right arm is held tight against the chest, and the elbow is sharply bent with the forearm held in a vertical position. With the palm of the right hand facing up, the back of the hand is held in a ninety-degree angle with the forearm (fig. 430).

The elbow of the left arm is extended in front of the left shoulder, held at a ninety-degree position. The two hands clasp forcefully (fig. 431). The right arm slowly pushes the left one forward by straightening the elbow quite a bit. At the same time that the clasped hands are pushed forward, the left shoulder and shoulder blade are also pushed forward to maintain the ninety-degree angle of the left elbow (fig. 432). The right arm retrieves the left hand to the initial position.

The clasped hands are shifted to the left side by pivoting on the palms, and the same movements are repeated there.

Figure 430

Figure 431

Figure 432

15. The Short Stab with the Hands Clasped

The hands are clasped at the right side, just as in the preceding magical pass. This time, however, the hands are at the level of the waist, and the right arm, instead of slowly pushing the left one forward, stabs fast (fig. 433). It is a powerful movement that requires the contraction of the muscles of the arms and the back. The clasped hands are brought forcefully to the left, as if to augment the driving force of the left elbow, which is pushed all the way to the back (fig. 434). The clasped hands move around the front of the body to the right, as if to aid again a powerful movement of the right elbow which is thrown all the way to the back.

Figure 433

Figure 434

The same sequence of movements is performed by starting it on the left side with the right hand in the lead.

It is important to note that when the clasped hands are stabbed to the front, the hand at the bottom gives the direction, but the force is supplied by the leading hand, which is on top.

16. Jolting Energy with Clasped Hands

The hands are clasped to the right; the right elbow and upper arm are held against the side of the rib cage. The elbow of the right arm is at a ninety-degree angle with the extended right forearm. The left elbow is also held at a ninety-degree angle, at a straight line away from the left pectoral muscle (fig. 435). The right arm lifts the left one, changing the position of the elbows from a ninety-degree angle to a forty-five. The clasped hands reach the level of the right shoulder (fig. 436). Then they are made to jolt with a very short movement in which only the wrist is involved. The clasped hands hit down, but without changing the level

Figure 435

Figure 436

Figure 437

Figure 438

at which they are held (fig. 437). From there, the clasped hands are retrieved to the left near the waist, in a forceful movement that makes the left elbow protrude at the back (fig. 438). The wrists are rotated and the hands made to pivot on each other, reversing their position. The same movements are repeated on the left.

17. Jolting Energy by the Knees

The hands are clasped to the right by the thigh. They change positions slightly by the supporting right hand, which is on the bottom, becoming slightly more vertical with a twist of the wrist, held in check by the pressure of the left hand (fig. 439). Both hands swing to the left, follow-

Figure 439

Figure 440

ing the contour of the knees, and deliver a strike, the potency of which is enhanced by a downward pull of the wrists (fig. 440).

The hands change position by rotating on each other's palms, and the same movements are repeated from left to right.

18. Driving Down a Spike of Energy

The hands are clasped vertically with the left hand in the lead, at a point about a foot from the navel, right on the division line between the left and right bodies. Both hands are lifted a few inches with a slight jolt made by bending the wrists without moving the forearms. Then they are brought down with the same jolt of the wrists (fig. 441).

This magical pass engages the deep muscles of the abdomen. The same movements are performed with the right hand in the lead.

Figure 441

19. Using the Hands Like a Hatchet

The hands are clasped at the right. Both are lifted to the level of the shoulder (fig. 442). Then they deliver a diagonal strike that takes them to the level of the left hip (fig. 443).

The same movements are done on the left.

Figure 442

Figure 443

20. Hammering a Spike of Energy

The hands are clasped at the right. They swing to the level of the shoulders, aided by a rotation of the trunk to the right. Making a small vertical circle in front of the right shoulder, the hands are brought to the division line between the two bodies and down to the level of the waist as if to hammer a spike of energy there (fig. 444).

The same movements are done on the left side.

Figure 444

The Third Group:
The Magical Passes for Building Endurance

Figure 445

21. Cutting Energy in an Arc

The hands are clasped on the right, tight against the crest of the hipbone. The left hand is on top of the right. The right elbow protrudes to the back, and the left forearm is held against the stomach. In a powerful extended strike, the clasped hands slice in a horizontal arc across the area in front of the body as if going through a heavy substance. It's as if the hands were holding a knife, or a sword, or a cutting instrument that rips something solid in front of the body (fig. 445). All the muscles of the arm, the abdomen, the chest, and the back are used. The muscles of the legs are tensed to lend stability to the movement. On the left side, the hands are pivoted. The right hand is on top, in the lead, and another powerful cut takes place.

22. Slashing Energy with a Swordlike Cut

The hands are clasped with the left hand on top of the right in front of the right shoulder (fig. 446). A powerful jolt of the wrists and the arms

Figure 446   *Figure 447*

makes the hands move forward about a foot, delivering a powerful blow. From there, they cut across to a point on the left, at the level of the shoulder. The end result is a movement that resembles cutting something heavy with a sword. From that point on the left, the arms change position by rotating, without losing their clasping position. The right hand takes the lead and gets on top, and again slashes across to a point about two feet away from the right shoulder (fig. 447).

The initial position of the hands are changed, and the movements begin on the left.

23. Slashing Energy with a Diagonal Cut

The clasped hands are raised to the level of the right ear and pushed forward, as if to stab something solid located in front of the body (fig. 448). From there, they slash down to a place about a foot away from the side of the left kneecap (fig. 449). On that point, the hands rotate at the wrists to change positions so that the right hand takes the lead on top. It is as if the cutting instrument that the hands seem to be holding is made to change directions before it slashes from left to right, following the contour of the knees (fig. 450).

Figure 448

The hands change place, and the whole sequence is done again, starting from the left.

Figure 449

Figure 450

24. Carrying Energy from the Right Shoulder to the Left Knee

The clasped hands are held at waist level on the right. They change positions slightly by the supporting right hand, which is on the bottom, becoming slightly more vertical with a twist of the wrist, which is held by the pressure of the left hand. The hands are quickly raised to a point by the top of the head, on the right side (fig. 451). Leading with the elbow, they are brought down to shoulder level with great force. From there, they slash down in a diagonal cut to a place about a foot away

Figure 451

Figure 452

from the left side of the kneecap. The strike is aided by a quick downward turn of the wrists (fig. 452).

The hands pivot to change places, and the whole sequence is done again, starting from the left.

25. Slashing Energy by the Knees

The hands are clasped on the right side by the waist (fig. 453). They are brought in a powerful downward strike to the level of the knees, as the trunk stoops forward slightly. Then they cut an arc in front of the knees from right to left, to a point four or five inches away from the left side of the kneecap (fig. 454). Then the clasped hands are brought back forcefully to a point a few inches to the right of the right knee. The performance of both cutting strikes is aided by a very powerful jolt of the wrists.

Figure 453   Figure 454

The same movement is performed starting by the waist on the left. In order to perform this magical pass correctly, practitioners need to engage, rather than the muscles of the arms and the legs, the deep muscles of the abdomen.

26. The Digging Bar of Energy

The clasped hands are held in front of the stomach, with the left hand on top as the leading hand. They are shifted then to a vertical position in front of the stomach on the line that separates the two bodies. In a quick movement, they are brought to a point above the head, as if still following the same line. From there, they are made to strike down in a straight line to the place where the magical pass began (fig. 455). The hands change positions, to have the right hand in the lead, and the movement is repeated. Don Juan called this movement *stirring energy with a digging bar*.

27. The Big Slash

The clasped hands start on the right, by the waist. They are quickly raised above the head, over the right shoulder (fig. 456). The wrists jolt back to gain strength, and a powerful diagonal strike is delivered that slashes energy in front of the body, as if cutting through a sheet. The strike ends at a point four or five inches to the left of the left knee (fig. 457).

Figure 455

The same movement is repeated starting from the left.

Figure 456

Figure 457

28. The Sledgehammer

With the left hand in the lead, the hands are clasped together in front of the stomach on the vertical line that divides the left and the right bodies. The palms are held vertical for an instant before the hands are brought to the right of the body and above the head to hang for another instant by the neck, as if holding a heavy sledgehammer. They move over the head in a deliberate and powerful swing (fig. 458) and are brought to bear on the spot from which they began to move, exactly as if the hands themselves were a heavy sledgehammer (fig. 459).

The hands change positions, and the same movements are started on the left.

Figure 458   Figure 459

29. Cutting a Circle of Energy

The hands are clasped by the right shoulder to begin this magical pass (fig. 460). Then they are pushed forward as far as the right arm can go without fully extending the elbow. From there, the clasped hands cut a circle the width of the body from right to left, as if they were indeed holding a cutting instrument. In order to perform this movement, the left, leading hand, which is on top, must reverse positions when it reaches the turn of the circle on the left; with the hands still clasped, they flip at the turn of the circle so that the right hand takes the lead by being on top (fig. 461) and finishes drawing the circle.

The same sequence of movements is performed, starting on the left, with the right hand in the lead.

Figure 460

Figure 461

30. The Back-and-Forth Slash

The hands are clasped on the right, with the left hand in the lead. A powerful blow pushes the hands forward, about two feet away from the chest. Then, they slash, as if they were holding a sword, as far to the left as the arms allow them without completely extending the elbows (fig. 462). There, the hands change positions. The right hand becomes the leading hand on top and a counterslash is performed, which takes the clasped hands all the way to a point on the right side, a few inches to the right of where this magical pass started (fig. 463).

The same sequence of movements is repeated, starting on the left, with the right hand in the lead.

Figure 462

Figure 463

Devices Used in Conjunction
with Specific Magical Passes

As previously stated, the shamans of ancient Mexico put a special emphasis on a force they called *tendon energy*. Don Juan said that they asserted that vital energy moves along the body via an exclusive track formed by tendons.

I asked don Juan if by *tendon* he meant the tissue that attaches the muscles to the bones.

"I am at a loss to explain *tendon energy*," he said. "I'm following the easy path of usage. I was taught that it's called *tendon energy*. If I don't have to be specific about it, you understand what *tendon energy* is, don't you?"

"In a vague sense, I think I do, don Juan," I said. "What confuses me is that you use the word *tendon* where there are no bones, such as the abdomen."

"The old sorcerers," he said, "gave the name of *tendon energy* to a current of energy that moves along the deep muscles from the neck down to the chest and arms, and the spine. It cuts across the upper and lower abdomen from the edge of the rib cage to the groin, and from there it goes to the toes."

"Doesn't this current include the head, don Juan?" I asked, bewildered. As a Western man, I expected that anything of this sort would have originated in the brain.

"No," he said emphatically, "it doesn't include the head. What comes from the head is a different kind of energetic current; not what I am talking about. One of the formidable attainments of sorcerers is that in the end, they push out whatever exists in the center of energy located at the top of the head, and then they anchor the *tendon energy* of the rest of their bodies there. But that is a paragon of success. At the moment, what we have at hand, as in your case, is the average situation of *tendon energy* beginning at the neck at the place where it joins the head. In some cases *tendon energy* goes up to a point below the cheekbones, but never higher than that point.

"This energy," he went on, "which I call *tendon energy* for lack of a better name, is a dire necessity in the lives of those who travel in *infinity*, or want to travel in it."

Don Juan said that the traditional beginning in the utilization of *tendon energy* was the use of some simple devices which were employed by the shamans of ancient Mexico in two ways. One was to create a vibratory effect on specific centers of *tendon energy*, and the other was to create a pressure effect on the same centers. He explained that those shamans considered the vibratory effect to be the agent for loosening the energy which has become stagnant. The second effect, the pressure effect, was thought to be the agent that disperses the energy.

What seems to be a cognitive contradiction for modern man—that vibration would loosen anything that was stuck, and that pressure would disperse it—was deeply emphasized by don Juan Matus, who taught his disciples that what appears to be natural to us in terms of our cognition in the world is not at all natural in terms of the flow of energy. He said that in the world of everyday life, human beings would crack something with a blow, or by applying pressure, and disperse it by making it vibrate. However, energy which had become lodged in a tendon center had to be rendered fluid through vibration, and then it had to be pressed, so that it would continue flowing. Don Juan Matus was horrified at the idea of directly pressing points of energy in the body without the preliminary vibration. His contention was that energy that was stuck would get even more inert if pressure were applied to it.

Don Juan started off his disciples with two basic devices. He explained that the shamans of ancient times used to search for a pair of round pebbles or dry round seed pods, and use them as vibratory and pressure devices to aid in manipulating the flow of energy in the body, which they believed becomes periodically stuck along the tendon track. However, the round pebbles that shaman practitioners normally used were definitely too hard, and the seed pods too fragile. Other objects that those shamans searched for avidly were flat rocks the size of the hand or pieces of heavy wood, in order to place them on specific areas of *tendon energy* on their abdomens while they were lying flat on their backs. The first area is just below the navel; another is right on top of the navel, and another yet, on the area of the solar plexus. The problem with using rocks or other objects is that they have to be heated or cooled to approximate the temperature of the body, and besides, these objects are usually too stiff, and they slide and move around.

Tensegrity practitioners have found a much better equivalent to the devices of the shamans of ancient Mexico: a pair of round balls and a small, flat, circular leather weight. The balls are the same size as the ones used by those shamans, but they are not fragile at all; they are made of a mixture of Teflon reinforced by a ceramic compound. This mixture gives the balls a weight, a hardness, and a smoothness which are thoroughly congruous with the purpose of the magical passes.

The other device, the leather weight, has been found to be an ideal device for creating a steady pressure on centers of *tendon energy*. Unlike rocks, it is pliable enough to adapt itself to the contours of the body. Its leather cover makes it possible to be applied directly to the body without needing to be warmed or cooled. However, its most remarkable feature is its weight. It is light enough not to cause any discomfort, and yet heavy enough to aid some specific magical passes that foster *inner silence* by pressing centers on the abdomen. Don Juan Matus said that a weight placed on any of the three areas mentioned above engages the totality of one's energy fields, which means a momentary shutting off of the *internal dialogue*: the first step toward *inner silence*.

The modern devices used in conjunction with specific magical passes are divided by their very nature into two categories.

The First Category

This first category of magical passes that use the help of a device consists of sixteen magical passes aided by the Teflon balls. Eight of these magical passes are performed on the left arm and wrist, and eight on the points of the liver and gallbladder, the pancreas and spleen, the bridge of the nose, the temples, and the crown of the head. The sorcerers of ancient Mexico considered the first eight magical passes to be the first step toward the liberation of the left body from the unwarranted dominion of the right body.

1. The first movement pertains to the outer side of the main tendon of the biceps of the left arm. A ball is applied to that hollow spot and made to vibrate by moving it back and forth with a slight pressure (figs. 464, 465).

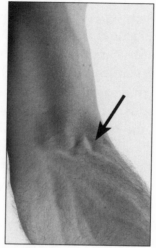

Figure 464

Figure 465

2. In the second movement, a ball is held in the hollow palm of the right hand, with the thumb holding it securely (fig. 466). A firm but light pressure is applied to the ball, which is made to rub from the left

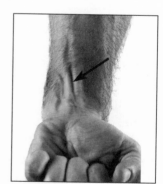

Figure 466

Figure 467

Figure 468

wrist to a point one hand's width away from the wrist (fig. 467). The ball is rubbed back and forth in the canal created by the tendons of the wrist (fig. 468).

3. The ball is lightly pressed at a point on the left forearm a hand's width away from the wrist (figs. 469, 470).

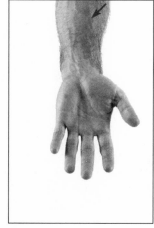

Figure 469

Figure 470

4. A moderate pressure is applied at the wrist of the left arm with the index finger of the right hand on a spot next to the head of the forearm bone (fig. 471). The right thumb anchors the hand on the inside of the wrist (fig. 472) and moves the hand back and forth (figs. 473, 474).

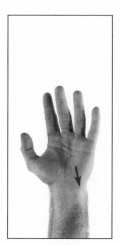

Figure 471

Figure 472

Figure 473

Figure 474

5. The ball is applied to the inner side of the tendon of the left biceps, and it is made to vibrate with a slight pressure (figs. 475, 476).

6. A vibration is applied to the hollow spot at the back of the elbow to the left of the elbow proper. The palm of the left hand is twisted and turned outward to allow maximum opening of that area (fig. 477). The ball is rubbed there.

Figure 475

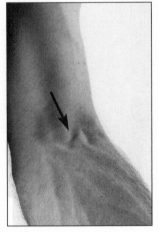

Figure 476

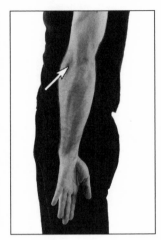

Figure 477

7. Moderate pressure is applied to a spot in the middle of the upper left arm, on the hollow spot where the triceps joins the bone (figs. 478, 479).

8. The left elbow is bent sharply and is rolled forward, engaging the left shoulder blade, to disperse tendon energy to the whole left body (fig. 480).

Figure 478

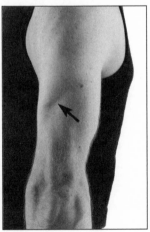

Figure 479

Figure 480

The remaining eight magical passes of this first category pertain to the upper body and three centers of energy: the gallbladder and liver, the pancreas and spleen, and the head.

9. The balls are held with both hands, pressed and pushed deeply upward, but with only slight pressure, just under the sides of the rib cage by the liver and the pancreas (fig. 481). Then they are made to vibrate firmly but lightly on those areas.

Figure 481

10. The ball held with the right hand is applied then with a slight pressure to the area just above the sinus, between the eyebrows, and is made to vibrate there (fig. 482).

Figure 482

11. Both balls are applied to the temples and made to vibrate lightly (fig. 483).

12. The ball held with the right hand is applied to the very top of the head and is made to vibrate there (fig. 484).

Figure 483   Figure 484

13–16. The same sequence is repeated, but instead of being made to vibrate, the balls are pressed against those centers of energy. During this second set of movements, both balls are pressed on the sides of the rib cage, by the liver and the pancreas. Then the ball held with the left hand is pressed on the area above the sinus. Both balls are pressed on the temples, and then the ball held with the left hand is pressed on the top of the head.

The Second Category

The second category comprises the uses of the leather weight for the purpose of creating a steady pressure on a larger area of *tendon energy*. There are two magical passes used in conjunction with the leather weight.

The hand positions for both of these magical passes are shown here with the practitioner standing. The actual practice of these magical passes is performed lying flat on the back with the leather weight pressing right above the navel or on either of the other two choice spots on the abdomen: below the navel, or above it by the solar plexus, if placing the weight on them is more comfortable.

Figure 485

17. The Five Points of Silence Around the Chest

The little fingers of both hands are placed on the edges of the rib cage about two inches from the tip of the sternum, and the thumbs are extended as far up on the chest as possible. The remaining three fingers fall evenly spread in the space between the thumb and the little finger. A vibratory pressure is exerted with all five fingers of each hand (fig. 485).

Figure 486

18. Pressing the Midpoint Between the Rib Cage and the Crest of the Hipbone

The little finger and the fourth finger of each hand rest on the crests of the hips while the thumbs rest on the lower edge of the rib cage on each side. Slight pressure is applied on those two points. The index and middle fingers automatically press points midway between the crests of the hips and the edge of the rib cage (fig. 486).

For information regarding seminars and workshops and videos on Carlos Castaneda's Tensegrity, contact:

Cleargreen Incorporated
11901 Santa Monica Boulevard, Suite 599
Los Angeles, California 90025
(310) 264-6126
Fax: (310) 264-6130
www.castaneda.com
cleargreen@castaneda.com

DON'T MISS THE 30TH ANNIVERSARY EDITION
OF CARLOS CASTANEDA'S CLASSIC BESTSELLER—
NOW WITH A NEW COMMENTARY
BY THE AUTHOR

CARLOS
CASTANEDA

THE TEACHINGS OF
DON JUAN:
A YAQUI WAY
OF KNOWLEDGE

This is the story of Carlos Castaneda's remarkable journey
into the unknown—in which he becomes the apprentice of a
Yaqui shaman named don Juan, and takes the first awesome
steps on the road to becoming a "man of knowledge."

"One can't exaggerate the significance of what
Castaneda has done." —*The New York Times*

Available wherever books are sold

WSP

WASHINGTON SQUARE PRESS
Published by Pocket Books